Starting Over

Using Torah and the Twelve Steps of Recovery to Find Happiness

By
Sima Devorah Schloss

Library of Congress Cataloging-in-Publication Data
Schloss, Sima Devorah, 1955-
Starting Over: Using Torah and The Twelve Steps of
Recovery to Find Happiness / by Sima Devorah Schloss
p. cm.
ISBN 1-880582-31-7
1. Schloss, Sima Devorah, 1955- —Religion. 2. Jews—United
States—Return to Orthodox Judaism. 3. Jewish way of life.
4. Twelve-step programs—Religious aspects—Judaism. I. Title.
BM205.S33 1998
296.7'15—dc21   CIP 98-33910

THE JUDAICA PRESS, INC.
123 Ditmas Avenue
Brooklyn, New York 11218
718-972-6200   800-972-6201
www.judaicapress.com • info@judaicapress.com

Manufactured in the United States of America

DEDICATED TO

the memories of my father and mother,

Melvin and Selma Kesselman, of blessed memory.

To my mother who was a model of goodness and

unconditional love & to my father

who always performed acts of loving kindness.

✦ ✦ ✦

To my aunts, Shirley Strum and Annette Stiglitz.

✦ ✦ ✦

To Rabbi Daniel Goldstein, of blessed memory,

who was a model of Torah.

✦ ✦ ✦

May all their souls benefit

from the merit of this book.

✦ ✦ ✦

Finally, I dedicate this book to the love of

my family, especially my husband, Robert,

my daughter, Ilana, my sister, Valerie Hale,

and my grandmother, Ruth Kesselman.

Table of Contents

Foreword

Never before has there been a time of diversity as extensive as today. Never before has there been a need for unification as desperate as our need is now. And unification, like diversity, can take many forms. In this book, Sima Schloss has successfully, with sensitivity and great clarity, brought together the disciplines of Jewish thought, of self-help groups, and of contemporary psychology–a remarkable feat and one that is deeply needed on all fronts.

In the section on Torah and the Twelve Steps, Mrs. Schloss explores the relation between "change" and *teshuva* (which means returning to the ways proclaimed by G–d). Without this connection, there might be no motivation for change. Concern for our physical and material lives alone fails to provide the direction, the meaning we all seek. However, by linking self-help work (the Twelve Steps) and Torah, we come to know what it means to grow as a spiritual being. In the

Biblical story of Cain and Abel, G-d teaches Cain that "...and to you is its desire, but you can rule over it" (Gen. 4:7). And Mrs. Schloss shows us that Twelve-Step meetings "are safe places where each person can feel accepted and supported." To implement the Biblical teachings, people meet in such groups to give and receive without fear of criticism.

Contemporary psychology, the third component, provides the specific characteristics of the codependent personality. This book includes a listing of nine separate questions that people can ask themselves to determine the degree of their codependency. For example: Do you usually consider everyone else's needs and ignore your own? Do you often say yes when you want to say no? And so on.

Mrs. Schloss closes her book with the reminder of the "baby steps" with which all serious self-work begins: May we all have the wisdom to strive to know God; May we all have the power to carry out G-d's will; May we all have the ability to say, "I choose life."

The ability to say, "I choose life" can be learned in the safe environment of the Twelve-Step group. The power to carry out G-d's will is given us in our study of Torah. The recognition of blockages that obstruct our innate potential for wisdom can be identified by the tools of contemporary psychology.

Here we have a unification of forces set forth in a book that fills a need long felt: *Starting Over.*

Dr. Blema Feinstein, 1997

Acknowledgements

With appreciation for the help and support of my teachers, Rabbis and friends: Rabbi Howard Diamond, Mr. Jeremy Litt, Mrs. Dianne Litt, Mrs. Kochava Sacks, Dr. Robin Bliss, Mrs. Zoey Saacks, and Mrs. Fran Diamond.

Thank you to Rabbi Jonathan Sacks for clarifying my ideas, Rabbi Yackov Saacks for his help with the Hebrew, Mr. Jonathan Ezor for his legal advice, Miss Golda Feinstein for being my first editor, Mr. Steve Roday for his help with chapter one, Mrs. Blema Feinstein for being my teacher, Rabbi Turk and Rabbi Portnoy of the Jewish Heritage Center for getting me started in Torah study.

Special thanks to Rachel Witty for knowing what I wanted to say and showing me how to say it better.

Special thanks to Bonnie Goldman and Judaica Press for believing in my book and pushing me to make it better. Thanks also to Zisi Berkowitz for her

beautiful book design and for her painstaking format-
ting of this book, and to Barbara Weinblatt for her
expert proofreading.

With deep gratitude to the *Rebono Shel Olam* for
giving me what I need and allowing me to complete
this project.

An Adaptation of the Twelve Steps

This is my adaptation of the classical Twelve Steps:

1. We admitted we were powerless over our own urges, and that our lives had become unmanageable.

2. Came to believe that a Power greater than ourselves could restore us to sanity.

3. Made a decision to turn our will and our lives over to the care of G-d, as we understood G-d.

4. Made a searching and fearless moral inventory of ourselves.

5. Admitted to G-d, to ourselves, and to another human being the exact nature of our wrongs.

6. Were entirely ready to have G-d remove all these defects of character.

7. Humbly asked G-d to remove our shortcomings.

8. Made a list of all persons we had harmed, and became willing to make amends to them all.

9. Made direct amends to such people wherever possible, except when to do so would injure them or others.

10. Continued to take personal inventory, and when we were wrong, promptly admitted it.

11. Sought through prayer and meditation to improve our conscious contact with G-d as we understood G-d, praying only for knowledge of G-d's will for us and the power to carry that out.

12. Having had a spiritual awakening as the result of these steps, we tried to carry this message to others, and to practice these principles in all our affairs.

The Original Twelve Steps of Alcoholics Anonymous

1. We admitted we were powerless over alcohol and that our lives had become unmanageable.

2. Came to believe that a Power greater than ourselves could restore us to sanity.

3. Made a decision to turn our will and our lives over to the care of G-d as we understood Him.

4. Made a searching and fearless moral inventory of ourselves.

5. Admitted to G-d, to ourselves and to another human being the exact nature of our wrongs.

6. Were entirely ready to have G-d remove all these defects of character.

7. Humbly asked Him to remove our shortcomings.

8. Made a list of all persons we had harmed, and became willing to make amends to them all.

9. Made direct amends to such people wherever possible, except when to do so would injure them or others.

10. Continued to take personal inventory, and, when we were wrong, promptly admitted it.

11. Sought through prayer and meditation to improve our conscious contact with G-d, as we understood Him, praying only for knowledge of His will for us and the power to carry that out.

12. Having had a spiritual awakening as the result of these steps, we tried to carry this message to alcoholics, and to practice these principles in all our affairs.

Prescription For A Better Life

Starting over means making a change. It won't be easy to change your life, but it will be worth the effort. This book contains a prescription for a better life. The instructions on this prescription are threefold:

1) **Learn Torah.** Before you can take action to change your life, you must have a clear mind and a set of guidelines. The best guidelines you can find any- where are the ones found in the Torah. But if this is the first time you're using the Torah in this way, you may have to ask yourself some questions:

♦ How can one know G–d and His ways?

♦ What does it mean to be a knowing or spiritual human being?

♦ What does it mean to live a life based on Torah?

Trying to answer these questions will start you in the right direction, but other questions will arise:

♦ How will you accomplish your goals?

✦ How will you institute the changes you desire?

As you proceed, more questions are sure to come up, but you must always keep in mind that to change your life you'll need a map and with Torah you will have a clear, sure direction.

2) **Take Twelve Steps.** Once you have a goal or direction, you need a method of implementation—a system of change. The Twelve Steps can help you make the changes you need and keep you on the path to a healthy life based on the wisdom of the Torah. Without Torah, your direction might not be clear and your progress to recovery may be hampered. Without a system of change like the Twelve Steps, you might not be able to get to where you need to go.

3) **Call G–d in the Morning.** Through prayer you can contact the Healer of healers. This is similar to when you are physically sick and you need to contact a doctor.

Prayer is simply turning to G–d for help. By reciting the formalized prayers written centuries ago, you are asking for the very things a person must have to live as a thinking, spiritual human being—one who is free to make choices based on knowledge of G–d and the world He created. Prayer is part of both the ways of Torah and the Twelve Steps, but it has its own singular importance because it is so often neglected. Success will be achieved only with G–d's help. You must find a way to forge a connection with G–d. Prayer can help you do this.

Learning Torah, following the Twelve Steps, and prayer are each important. Taken individually, they might not be enough to institute the changes that you need. Together, they are a powerful combination for anyone who is struggling to change.

You may still be thinking:

✦ Do I really need this information?

✦ Will I really benefit from this prescription?

✦ Is this system for me?

I wrote this book to share my discovery with others who are dissatisfied with their lives, and would like to change.

Combining Torah study with the Twelve Steps is an excellent system for *baalei teshuva*, i.e., newly observant Jews who are in the process of changing various aspects of their lives. However, this powerful combination can also help anyone, observant Jew or not, who wants to improve individual character traits.

Thus, if you are observant of Jewish law, but unfamiliar with the Twelve Steps or if you are already working the Twelve Steps, but are unsure about your commitment to Judaism or if you just want to be free of your own unhealthy habits, and are open to the possibilities of change, this book is for you.

Following a Torah–based lifestyle or working a Twelve–Step program are each big commitments. The combination may seem overwhelming. No drastic measures are required. Even small changes can help to move you in a healthier direction. Many people work a long time on one step before moving on, and this is perfectly fine since this is how the system works. You work on what you feel you can do. There is no set order or timetable. You can go back and forth between the steps as needed or as desired. I have not worked very much on Steps Eight and Nine, but I have worked a lot on Step Eleven and I often go back to work on Steps One through Three.

Neither the Twelve Steps, nor this book, is a magical formula. Simply reading about the Steps will not change anyone. Doing *teshuva* is an ongoing process. *Teshuva* means getting rid of habits that are leading you in the wrong direction and replacing these habits with deliberate actions that will lead you toward G-d. Discard and replace. Change direction.

Change is hard work. Torah concepts and many of the suggestions in this book must be constantly reviewed. Read, reread, and discuss them over and over again. Work and rework the Twelve Steps. Pray each day.

The Twelve Steps provide a system in which I can organize the Torah's teachings about *teshuva*. I have improved my understanding of G-d's existence and power and I have increased my ability to turn to G-d for help, by working Steps One through Three. Steps Four through Seven gave me a working structure for improving my character traits. Working Step Eleven helped me learn how to personalize my prayers and

ask G–d for help. If you follow this path, you are head-
ed for a lifetime of hard work; however, the outcome,
is well worth the effort.

I am a *baalat teshuva* and a recovering codependent. I feel very grateful to Hashem that I was given
the opportunity and the wisdom to adopt a Torah-
based life and to find the Twelve-Step system of
recovery. My life has acquired meaning and purpose.
By focusing my energies on attaining meaningful
goals, I have improved my health and increased my
happiness. This book is my attempt to give that
opportunity and wisdom to others who need it.

I am asking you to open your mind and your
heart.

◆ Do you want to change?

◆ Do you want to be happy?

◆ Do you want to be free of your own bad habits?

◆ Are you ready to consider working for a better
and healthier lifestyle?

Change could come rather quickly, or it could take
years of hard work. I will share with you what I have
discovered. With G–d's help, you will discover exactly
what *you* need to free yourself so you can step forward toward a happier more satisfied life.

My Story

The reasons that I turned my life upside down at the age of thirty-four—becoming both an Orthodox Jew and joining a Twelve-Step program are neither dramatic nor extraordinary. I did not suffer any traumatic experiences. I grew up in a loving family and now have a wonderful family of my own.

As a child, I attended Sunday school in a Reform synagogue, and services on Friday nights. We celebrated the Jewish holidays, and I was proud of being Jewish, but I was given no concept of binding commandments given by G-d. Even though I always enjoyed learning about Judaism, it never occurred to me to do anything more.

Searching for Happiness

Perhaps the most traumatic event of my childhood happened when I was sixteen, and my cousin, Ezra, an epileptic who otherwise was perfectly healthy, suddenly developed a blood clot in his brain. He lapsed into a coma, and as a result, suffered severe brain damage. Ezra was a married man in his early thirties and the father of two children. For months we would pack up the car with food every Friday and visit his family in the Bronx. I would sit in the car with my mother, aunt, sister, and cousin, and take in the aroma of baked chickens emanating from the trunk. We would visit Ezra in the hospital, leave the food for his family and return to Long Island. After awhile, he was moved to a rehabilitation center nearby. Then his family came to us. We set up a crib for the baby. When they could do no more for him, Ezra was transferred to a county nursing home, where my aunt visited faithfully every week until she died. To this day, Ezra remains in this home. He is blind and sits all day in a wheelchair. His brain has healed to the extent that he knows enough to be unhappy, but he will never get better.

As a result of this tragedy, all the things that everyone else thought were fun or important lost their interest for me. I became angry with G-d and threw Him out of my life. As I got older, I searched for something that would add meaning to my life, but I could never find exactly what I needed. Music was my first love, and I found comfort playing piano and studying music.

After graduating from college, I visited Israel. The trip helped me feel more connected to being Jewish, and I felt strongly about marrying someone Jewish. A few weeks after my return from Israel, I met the man who would become my husband. He came from a Conservative Jewish family and wanted to keep a kosher home, so we did. After a year and a half, my husband signed a contract for work which brought us back to Israel. It was there that I learned Hebrew and more about how to keep a kosher kitchen. We lived on Kibbutz Ketura. Ketura is a unique *kibbutz* because it accepts all people, regardless of their beliefs. The individual members include observant, non-observant, and secular Jews. As a community, Ketura observes both Shabbat and the laws of keeping kosher. My bond to Judaism strengthened in the two and a half years that we spent in Israel.

Exploring My Heritage

When we returned to New York in 1982, I taught in the afternoons at a Reform synagogue. One of my responsibilities was to teach the weekly Torah portion to classes of fourth-, fifth-, and sixth-grade students. The more I prepared for each class, the more I wanted to know. In the fall of 1988 I attended classes offered by the Jewish Heritage Center of Queens. Rabbi Portnoy, who was in charge, sent me to learn with a small group of women led by Dr. Blema Feinstein, Professor Emeritus of C.W. Post College, Long Island University. Dr. Feinstein is both a Torah counselor and teacher of Jewish women newly motivated by their enthusiasm for Torah life. She teaches privately and through organizations such as the

Jewish Heritage Center. By the end of Dr. Feinstein's first class, I was inspired. She was able to combine the beauty of Torah with the idea that learning can help one's personal growth and development. Dr. Feinstein's teachings impressed me because they related to me both as a Jew and as a woman. With her help, I developed a passion for Torah Judaism. Dr. Feinstein has remained both my teacher and mentor ever since that first meeting in 1988.

Soon after I began learning with Dr. Feinstein, I noticed how frequently Shabbat is mentioned in the Torah. Just going to services on Friday nights didn't seem enough for something that seemed to be a key to being Jewish. It certainly bore no resemblance to the Shabbat that was mentioned in the Torah. I felt drawn to the idea of this day of complete rest and dedication to G–d.

First, I stopped doing laundry and going shopping, making Shabbat more of a family day. Then I began to light candles and make chicken soup for dinner. Shabbat evolved slowly in our home. By the spring of 1989, I made a commitment to fully observe Shabbat, including all the laws—for example I stopped driving, carrying, adjusting electric devices, or answering the telephone. This was a turning point in my acceptance of the Torah as a way of life. My life became more imbued with the Torah ideas that I had been learning. Once I began to observe Shabbat, I slowly added other *mitzvot* (commandments) into my life, such as observing all of the holidays and fast days, covering my hair, and putting kosher *mezuzot* on all of the doorposts of my house.

My daughter was only four when I began to observe these Torah laws. She accepted the changes naturally, as if our lives had always been that way. For her, Shabbat meant more quality time with Mommy. The changes were not as easy for my husband. At first, they were only my changes. Being stricter about keeping kosher in the house was not a problem for him. I tried not to ask my husband what he ate out of the house. My daughter and I began to walk to *shul* (synagogue) together on Shabbat mornings. Eventually my husband joined us. He would say he liked to walk and was concerned about our walking alone. I did what I had to do about being observant, and I tried not to question him. This is one area where I believe I have acted in a healthy way. Our commitment to each other allowed us to give each other some space but still stay together.

My husband was often amazed and not always pleased about the changes that I brought into our household, but, thank G–d, I am proud to say we have remained married. An unhappy wife does not make a happy marriage. In the long run, I think my husband sees the benefits that Torah has brought to our marriage and family. Some of the changes have been difficult for him to accept. We try to communicate and compromise with each other. He doesn't like the hats that many Orthodox women wear to cover their hair. So I bought some stylish caps and a quality wig.

Learning the Torah and doing the *mitzvot* changed my life by giving me new goals and a new direction. I found that by attaining a greater knowledge of G–d, doing His will, and by being satisfied with what He has given me I was finding a way to a happier life. I use the phrase "way to a happier life," because even with all the dramatic changes in my life—keeping Shabbat for the very first time, following stringent kosher laws, learning Torah, and doing *mitzvot*—even with these changes, I still was not content. My learning was unfocused and my goals were unclear. The ideas were not integrated into my life in a way that would give me a sense of peace or happiness. Although I was surely heading in the right direction, I could not seem to get to where I needed to be.

My life was good. There were no tragedies, no awful people complicating my life. I had only my share of the normal stresses—work, the house, and family members who needed me. The death of my aunt, and then my mother, were big personal blows, but certainly something others experience as well. My father moved in with us for about nine months, but still there were only four people in my household.

I was trying to be a better Jew and a better person, but the everyday demands of life often overwhelmed me. I did not have any more problems than anyone else. Maybe, I had even fewer problems. So, why was I still unhappy?

Searching for Myself

I gradually discovered that I was unhappy because I couldn't stop taking care of everyone. I was the habitual helper. My giving to others was the result of feeling that I had to, instead of deliberately making a choice. I really did not know enough to understand the Torah concepts of *chesed* (kindness) and *tzedaka* (charity). I did not understand that I was not supposed to help others if it meant harming myself.

I felt that I could save or help everyone, if only I tried: When my mother became ill, I read case studies in the hospital library about her type of cancer. Although there's nothing inherently wrong with that, I took on the responsibility for her staying alive. When she died in 1992, for a long time I believed that she might still be alive if only I had found the right cure for her in time.

After my mother died my father moved in with us. I was working two days a week as a special education music teacher, and there always seemed to be so much to do—I never knew what to do first. I would be preparing a meal and worrying that I should be spending my time sending out resumes for a better job. If I went on an interview, I would think about how my poor cousin Ezra could really use a visit now that his regular visitors—my mother and aunt—were no longer

alive. I would travel to Manhattan to see my grandmother, all the while worrying about returning home
in time for my daughter. Even though my husband's
office was in the house, I felt that my daughter really
needed me to be there when she arrived home from
the local yeshiva. While doing the laundry, I worried
that perhaps my husband needed my help; so I would
help my husband and feel anxious about the house
being a mess. Somehow, I had turned the act of giving
into a way to control other people, to buy friends, and
to feel accepted. I found that I could feel good about
myself as long as I could help someone else.

Even though I was always ready to help others, I
could never ask others for help. I felt I could do
everything better, and, in addition, I didn't want to
bother anyone. When I felt overburdened, I resented
my family for not offering assistance. Yet how could
they help me? I had made it clear that their help
would never be good enough.

That was my life in 1993. I was so busy taking care
of everyone else that I found no time to take care of
myself. Six years after our first meeting, I confessed to
Dr. Blema Feinstein how busy and stressed I was.

Dr. Feinstein listened to me rush on about how
overwhelmed I was and how I took care of everyone.
She immediately said, "You need CoDA (Codependents
Anonymous)." She saw that I had lost myself in the
role of taking care of everyone else. She made me
aware of the ideas of codependency and the Twelve

Steps of recovery.

I resisted. Why would someone like me need the Twelve Steps? I already had Torah. Besides, weren't the Twelve Steps for people addicted to drugs or alcohol? Soon I came to see that my own bad habits and codependent characteristics were causing my unhappiness. I will forever be grateful to her because she helped me discover both the Torah and Codependents Anonymous. And I discovered that the Twelve Steps helped me make a stronger commitment to Torah Judaism. The combination of Twelve Steps and Torah makes for a powerful mix.

What is
Codependents Anonymous?

I **went to my first Codependents Anonymous** meeting because I figured I had nothing to lose, and my trusted teacher and friend had told me to try it. She had helped me with Torah, so perhaps she could now help me with this problem. I was nervous and uncomfortable at the meetings—all the more so because most of the meetings were held in church meeting rooms. (This could be a *halachic* (Jewish legal) problem, so before you attend a meeting you may want to consult your rabbi.) When I first heard people in the meeting talk about addiction and abuse in their families, I wondered if I had made a mistake. My background was nothing like theirs, or so I thought. I began to think that maybe Dr. Feinstein was wrong and I wasn't really a codependent after all.

Someone in the group advised me to attend three meetings before I decided if it was for me. I continued going at first only because I left each meeting knowing a little more about myself and feeling a little better. It wasn't until many months had passed before I finally admitted to myself and to others that I was a codependent.

A Safe Place To Change

If you've never been to a Twelve-Step meeting you may wonder what they are like. They are like any other kind of meeting—people gather in a room—the difference is they are safe places where each person can feel accepted and supported. The ground rules are different—people can give and receive kindness, without fear of being criticized or exploited—important for someone who is a habitual helper or perfectionist. Whatever is said is heard free of judgment and in anonymity. At each meeting we state, "What is said here, let it remain here." Nobody is allowed to preach or give advice. Each person tells his or her story from the heart.

I learned a surprising thing from listening to others at CoDA meetings. I learned that there are both healthy and unhealthy ways of giving. When the giving is good for both the giver and the receiver, it is healthy. It is unhealthy when it is harmful to either the giver or the receiver. Giving can be wonderful, or it can be controlling and manipulative.

Codependent people feel compelled to give in ways that are not healthy. I began to understand that a codependent is someone whose life choices and decisions are based upon the thought, speech, and action of others to such an extent that the codependent no longer considers her or his own needs or feelings. The codependent's actions revolve around another person. The focus is on changing or controlling someone else.

Codependents adjust their lives in an attempt to save others from their addictions or from bad habits. For instance, a codependent might be reluctant to leave the house to insure that an alcoholic is not drinking or that an overeater is not indulging in food. Codependents automatically say yes to many demands and responsibilities, so that no one will get angry or depressed, or be provided with an excuse to drink, take drugs, eat, or get into an angry rage.

Characteristics of Codependents

How can you determine if you are a codependent? Consider some of the following questions:

✦ Do you often say yes when you really want to say no?

✦ Do you usually consider everyone else's needs first and ignore your own?

✦ Do you consistently neglect your needs because you feel there isn't any time for them?

✦ Do you feel that you must be the one to perform most tasks even when others are available?

✦ Do you always see the potential in others and spend a great deal of your energy in getting them to change?

✦ Do you try to make everything perfect—your job, house, vacation, dinner, conversation, friends, family, and yourself?

✦ Do you feel compelled to help your spouse or children with their choice of clothes, friends, activities, food, work, even when they seem quite able to do it by themselves?

✦ Do you feel responsible and/or guilty for many things that go wrong with friends or family, that somehow you may be responsible for their flaws, mistakes, unhappiness, failure, bad habits, or addictions?

✦ Do you feel an overwhelming need to be needed?

Most codependents would answer yes to the majority of these questions. In 1993, I would probably have answered yes to all of them.

Finding Myself

With G–d's help and Dr. Feinstein's assistance, I found recovery. Recovery is a word that signifies changing from a state of sickness to a state of health. It is a process of getting better. In the Twelve–Step system, recovery means changing from reacting through harmful habits to making deliberate choices for a healthier life.

Following the Steps is commonly called "Working The Steps" which is a Twelve Step idea that involves both learning about The Steps and acting according to The Steps. Learning can come in the form of reading books and literature on the Twelve Steps as well as attending Step meetings organized in order to review the Steps. Some Twelve Step meetings review one Step each month. When people speak at meetings, they may discuss one particular Step and how it helps them to better their lives. The more you understand each Step, the more you can put them into action. The more you put them into action—like remembering that you are not in control, accepting G–d's will and asking forgiveness for wrongdoings—the more you can utilize the Steps. Working the Steps is a continuous process of learning, acting and integrating the Steps into your life.

My timing was a blessing. Before I even found the Twelve Steps, I had begun to build a relationship with G–d. It turned out that the basis of the Twelve Steps is acknowledging a Power greater than you. So, by finding and observing the Torah, by working the Twelve Steps, and with lots of prayer, I was able to really begin my recovery and step into freedom. It took almost two years of working the Twelve Steps before I noticed the healthy improvements in my life. After taking care of others for so long, I was finally beginning to find myself. My physical condition is much better; I joined a martial arts program; I try to walk every day; I have a job I love; and I continue to learn Torah with other women on a regular basis.

My daughter is growing and enjoying her new found independence. When I stopped trying to control her, I discovered that I had a responsible daughter who is sensible about making her own decisions—homework, sick days from school, clothing, and leisure activities. Our relationship improved, too, when I refrained from nagging her to do things my way. I have learned to love her for who she is.

My relationship with my husband is also better. I now appreciate him for his wonderful qualities, instead of focusing on ways he could improve.

The Torah and the Twelve Steps

My investigation for this book began because I wanted to make sure the Twelve-Step system fit in with Torah, which had become the foundation and guide in my life. A system of change which was not in line with Torah principles had become unacceptable to me.

The Hebrew word *teshuva* signifies change and return to the ways of G-d and the Torah. A need to return implies a loss of direction. Through preoccupation with physical or material existence, we may lose the path to our essential human life as spiritual beings who can think and make intelligent choices. For Jews, the essence of spirituality is searching for what is right through knowledge of G-d and knowledge of Torah.

The Torah will not automatically give you freedom or happiness. By observing the *mitzvot*, you actuate the potential to affect your personal characteristics, and free yourself from your own flaws, but there is no guarantee.

It is possible to observe the laws of keeping kosher by rote, without even giving a thought about G–d as the Author of these laws and without understanding that by observing these laws you are doing His will. You can strictly observe Shabbat and have a day of rest without increasing your knowledge of G–d or using the day to train yourself to be satisfied with what He has given you. You have to consciously make an effort to be transformed by following the Torah. However, sometimes even if you are aware of the changes that you'd like to institute, they may not occur.

For me, finding happiness means increasing my knowledge of G–d, doing what He wants, and being satisfied with what He gives me. By studying Torah, I have learned that I can always turn to G–d for help. As a Jew, I have built my relationship with G–d and increased my reliance on Him every day by praying and by doing what He commands. Two of the basic principles of the Twelve Steps instruct us to rely on a Power greater than ourselves and to make His will our will. These are also basic principles of the Torah. The Twelve Steps can set us on a path of *teshuva* or return to our own essential human selves and ultimately toward the greater Power in the world that we know as G–d. With the Torah pointing to the right path, the steps become a powerful tool to create a healthier and happier life.

One truth does not conflict with another. Following Torah is not only compatible with, but adds strength to, practicing the Twelve Steps. As a rabbi once told me, "The Twelve Steps are Torah."

One can be influenced to change when one truly opens one's heart and relates to another human being's story. This is very different from being lectured at or being given advice. To influence someone with words from the heart is a Torah idea. To affect others by sincerely telling your story is a Twelve-Step idea. We change ourselves when we are ready to ask G–d for His assistance.

The Twelve-Step Program

So now that you know more about what code-pendency is and have discovered the relationship between the Twelve Steps and the Torah, you may be wondering what exactly are these Twelve Steps.

The first Twelve-Step program was co-founded in 1935 in Akron, Ohio, by two alcoholics, a New York broker and a surgeon. They were determined to help themselves and other alcoholics. After three years of observing others, they combined their information with ideas from religion and medicine to formulate the basic principles of the Twelve Steps, and they established three successful groups. In 1939 they wrote a book they called *Alcoholics Anonymous*, which gave the fellowship its name and codified the Twelve Steps.

The meetings became safe places where recovering alcoholics could share their stories without fear of criticism, where the story of one would penetrate the heart of another. The people who looked to Alcoholics Anonymous felt that their lives were desperately unmanageable. The steps and meetings worked.

Alcoholics Anonymous grew in size and in respectability. The AA fellowship can be found today worldwide in more than 130 countries. There are also many other Twelve-Step groups, including Codependents Anonymous, which bases its meetings on the original Twelve Steps and Thirteen Principles of Alcoholics Anonymous.

The original Twelve Steps of recovery is much more than a way out of a dependency or an addiction. It is an effective system for anyone struggling to change. People do not look for a system of change unless they feel desperate. To find a solution, a person must admit there is a problem. It took me years to recognize that I had one.

I turned to the Twelve Steps of Codependents Anonymous (CoDA) and found keys to a healthier life. The Twelve Steps gave me a specific, concrete, step-by-step structure that I could use to apply Torah principles to my life. I found that what I learned was so incredible and so fulfilling that I wanted to share this prescription for a happier life with others. I pray that you can find the strength to make whatever changes are necessary to improve your life and that you find these Steps as helpful as I have.

Learning Torah

The *foundation of all the work we are about to* undertake is learning Torah. Before we begin going through the Twelve Steps, I'll delve into why learning Torah is important and how this will set the tone for each and every part of your life. Plus, you'll begin to learn why the combination of Torah and Twelve Steps makes for a system of change that really works. As we find in Psalms (128:1–2):

"Happy is anyone who fears G–d, who walks in His ways. When you eat from the labor of your hands you will be happy and it will be good for you ."

The psalm promises that I will be happy and have a good life, if I fear G–d, do His will, and am satisfied with what I have. The proverb "Happy is the person who finds wisdom" (Proverbs 3:13) further assures me that I will be happy when I find wisdom. The Torah is filled with wisdom that teaches us about G–d and what He wants us to do.

When I began to learn Torah, I did not expect it to make me happy. After all, at the beginning I was simply teaching Bible stories to my students. To my surprise, I was drawn in by these stories and I wanted to learn more. What did it all mean? Why was Shabbat mentioned so often?

Before I realized it, I had fallen in love with Judaism. I discovered that the Torah is much more than an accumulation of stories. Both the written and oral traditions contain wisdom, beautiful concepts, and lofty ideals. Torah, I finally understood, is actually a guide for a fulfilled life and an improved world.

Free Will and Making Changes

Learning led to change. I began to observe Shabbat and other mitzvot. The Torah gave my existence a purpose. It provided me with some clarity and insight into G–d's will.

I made a free-will choice to let the Torah guide me to a better life, because I fell in love with the Torah's teachings about what life should be like. I decided to try to follow this guide before I even understood that it would make me happier. Now I search for wisdom because I want to fear G–d, walk in His ways, and be satisfied with what He gives me.

The great Jewish thinker Rambam (Maimonides) explained that every human being has free will. We all can make choices between what is right and what is wrong, what is good and what is evil. We can all decide which way to direct our lives.

As Rambam writes, free will is given to everyone. The power is in one's hand if one desires to turn towards the good way and be righteous. We have similar power, if one wishes, to turn towards the evil way and be wicked. Rambam points out that it is written, "Behold, the man has become as one of us, to know good and evil" (Genesis 3:22). Rambam says this means that humans had become unique in the world—a human, individually, and by the exercise of one's own intelligence and reason, knows what is good and what is evil, and nothing can prevent one from doing what is good or evil (Hilchot Teshuva 5:1).

A human being is born good and pure, with the ability to do what is right. Although we may have some inborn dispositions, Rambam explains that we definitely have free will. Each of us can choose good or evil, right or wrong. However, each choice is accompanied by a whole set of circumstances.

When we make the wrong choices, we continue to go further down the wrong path, often reaching a point from which it becomes impossible to return by sheer willpower. Anyone who has become accustomed to harmful activities, such as overeating, drinking, or smoking knows how difficult it is to change by merely deciding to do so. It usually takes many attempts and failures to change before the person finds a system that works.

Through our free will we continue searching for a

solution to our problems, even when we feel power-less to overcome them. Our free will allows us to keep trying to change for the good, even when it appears overwhelmingly difficult.

Searching for Happiness

At times, I chose the wrong path. My instincts to control others were very powerful and I followed them. The more I chose to do this, the more difficult it became to make the right choice. I got further and further away from truth and knowledge. My thinking became more and more distorted.

For example, by trying to control the lives of my husband, daughter, father, and mother, I lost track of myself. I could not leave things for others to do. I always believed that no one could do them as per-fectly as I could. There was no time to take care of myself either physically or spiritually.

Although I knew that I wanted to change, I felt powerless, but I searched for answers to my unhappi-ness. My choice was to pursue knowledge of G–d.

I began my search for a healthier and happier life by learning Torah. Learning Torah directed me to the right path for a happier life. I believe it can help any-one who is searching for a better way to live.

As Proverbs (4:7) states: "The beginning of wis-dom is: get wisdom." The source of all wisdom is G–d. So, the beginning of happiness is learning about G–d and building a relationship with Him.

Seeking G-d

G-d communicates with us in the Torah. In reading the Torah and in our attempt to understand His words, we strive to know Him. But when we try to understand the world—G-d's creation—we also improve our knowledge of G-d.

In much of his writings, Rambam details and explains how the universe works, recognizing that it is through our knowledge of G-d's creation that we can come to perceive G-d. Rambam discusses the physical world, the heavenly sphere, and angels, and notes that each of us will be attracted to different aspects of the universe.

Rambam, in *Mishne Torah*, explains that the reason he describes some general aspects of G-d's works, is so that "they may serve as a door to loving G-d. As our sages have remarked in connection with the theme of the love of G-d, 'Observe the universe and you will recognize Him Who spoke and the world was'" (Hilchot Yesodei HaTorah 2:2).

Everyone must discover his or her own door to G-d. It will not be the same entrance for everyone. In my searching I kept coming up against a blank wall. I read books and attended lectures and seminars. Some people seemed to be convinced of G-d's existence and involvement in the world as the logical conclusion of scientific and historical information. This approach did not convince me.

My door to belief and faith in G–d came as a result of my focus and interest in people and relationships. I began to see the wisdom of the Torah system because of its positive effects on me, on other people, and on relationships. Only then did I begin to recognize and love the Creator of this wisdom.

Following the laws of marriage and family purity has brought me closer to my husband. By learning to accept and understand my husband better, I appreciate him more on both a physical and intellectual level. I can see the benefits of my daughter's yeshiva education. Her values are clear because her education focuses on the values of the Torah. By following the commandments, I have become a more patient person and a more effective wife, mother, teacher and recreational therapist.

My ability to think and understand things and how I choose to speak and act upon that knowledge is my essence as a person. The ability to know what is right and then make a free choice is uniquely human. It is what sets human beings apart from the rest of the physical world.

Thinking and figuring things out can give us tremendous pleasure. Why else would some people spend hours playing a game of chess? It is the joy of utilizing the powers of the mind that students feel when they complete a difficult paper or project.

My greatest pleasure in life comes from using this special ability that G–d gave us. This ability enables us to know G-d better and to understand His ways in our lives and the ways of the world. I grow closer to Him and connect myself to His wisdom when I can recognize His ways in myself and in the world.

I purposely act with more patience or kindness because I know that it is a characteristic of G-d which I am supposed to emulate as a Jew. When I see the benefits that I have from trying to follow a life that is based on Torah, His ways in my life are being revealed.

I taught the Torah portion of the week in an afternoon Hebrew school. The children asked me why G-d was always present in the Torah but seemed invisible today. G-d is present, I explained but we must train ourselves to see Him. Iraq bombed Israel during the Gulf War with little damage to human life. Many people saw this as good luck or a chance event. Others saw the hand of G-d. The difference was in the perceiver and not in G-d.

I try to mentally connect myself to G-d by attaching myself to His wisdom and to His will. By following the commandments of the Torah and by trying to emulate His ways in my life, I heighten my awareness of G-d. When I say a blessing before I eat, I bring G-d to my dinner table. I can give charity simply because it is a good thing and it makes me feel good to help others. But by giving charity with an awareness that this is one of G-d's commandments, I bring G-d into my consciousness.

The first book in Rambam's *Mishne Torah* is Sefer Hamadah, The Book of Knowledge. Here Rambam informs us that the foundation of wisdom and belief is acknowledging G–d's existence—acknowledging that G–d created the world and continuously sustains the world.

Rambam says: "The basic principle of all basic principles and the pillar of all wisdom is to know that there is a First Being Who brought everything that exists into being. All things exist only through His true existence" (*Mishne Torah*, Hilchot Yesodei HaTorah 1:1).

Through Torah and through logic we can know that G–d exists. However, we are part of the physical world. G–d is not physical. Our minds are limited by our physicality, and thus it is impossible for us to grasp the precise nature of G–d. As Rambam tells us:

"G–d's essence, as it really is, the human mind does not understand and is incapable of grasping or investigating" (*Mishne Torah*, Hilchot Yesodei HaTorah 1:9).

Even Moshe, our greatest prophet, could not completely understand G–d. He could catch only a glimpse of G–d, similar to recognizing someone by seeing only his back. Moshe yearned to sharpen his perception of G–d, but he was told that it is humanly impossible to know more.

Rambam asks: "What was it that Moshe sought to comprehend, when he asked G–d, 'Show me, I beseech You, Your glory?' (Exodus 33:18). Moshe was attempting to understand the truth of G–d's existence so that

knowing G–d would be like distinguishing one person
from another by having seen a face and having the
features imprinted on the mind. Moshe, our teacher,
searched for knowledge of G–d's existence so that He
would be so distinguished from other beings that
Moshe would comprehend the truth of G–d's existence as it really is. G–d replied that it is impossible
for humans, who are made of body and soul, to know
the truth as it really is. However, G–d gave Moshe
knowledge which no human before or after him
would ever know. Moshe comprehended the truth
of G–d's existence to the extent that his mind was
able to distinguish G–d's existence from other beings
like an individual who is distinguished from others
when his back is seen, by recognizing his physical
form and shape" (*Mishne Torah*, Hilchot Yesodei
HaTorah 1:10).

I have learned that although there will always be
a limit to my knowledge of G–d, I can strive to know
more.

As a child, I pictured G–d as an old man with a
long white beard, sitting up in the clouds. My image
was one of a superhuman being, but a human being
nonetheless. Learning Torah pushed me past this concept of G–d "made in man's image." Now I know that
I cannot have a physical image of G–d. To know G–d
as I know another person or any physical being is
beyond my mental capacity as a human being. I can
only know that G–d exists by seeing His work in our

physical world. It is possible to know what He does, *not* what He is.

Love and Fear of G-d

Once I acknowledged G-d's existence, I still wasn't sure how I could relate to Him. In the *Mishne Torah*, Rambam informs us that we are commanded to feel both love and fear of G-d. How could I love and fear something or someone that I could not see, hear, or touch?

As I have mentioned, Rambam tells us to observe G-d's creations, which I can see, hear, and touch. By appreciating the wisdom and beauty of the natural world, by loving the creation, I can come to love the Creator. I can begin to feel awe and fear for the immense power and wisdom behind His creations.

"And what way will lead to the love and fear of G-d?" Again Rambam says that "when one contemplates G-d's great and wondrous works and creatures and has the opportunity to obtain a glimpse of His incomparable and infinite wisdom, one will immediately love Him, praise Him, glorify Him and long to know His great Name" (*Mishne Torah*, Hilchot Yesodei HaTorah 2:2).

Knowing G-d's great Name means recognizing G-d's attributes and wisdom in the world. When I see someone act kindly or see an example of goodness, I make an effort to understand it as a manifestation of G-d's kindness and goodness. When I am saved from a dangerous situation, I try to perceive it as experiencing G–d's mercy. A walk outside is an opportunity to contemplate the wisdom behind natural phenomena. The existence of such wondrous creations necessitates the existence of a Creator.

I do not want to stay in G–d's doorway, simply acknowledging His existence. I want to go into His house, so that I can learn to love and fear Him. I read, pray, go to lectures, and learn with others.

To know G–d better, I had to take the ideas from learning and start to experience and recognize them in my life. Events do not happen by luck or chance. G–d had, in fact, been guiding my life towards Him all the time. Only recently had I started to perceive it.

Once my perception changed, I noticed how people and circumstances have helped to move my life in the direction of Torah and G–d. I connected all the pieces of my life puzzle.

My childhood gave me a love of learning and Judaism. Although we did not observe Jewish law in my family, my mother took us to services every Friday night, and we celebrated all the Jewish holidays. I was always encouraged and supported in my academic studies, both Jewish and secular. Visiting Israel gave me an urgency to marry a Jewish man and build a Jewish home. My husband brought the laws of kosher food into our home when we were first married. Teaching in an afternoon Hebrew school brought me to the importance of following the commandments of the Torah.

Following the commandments of the Torah has led me
to searching for G–d.

Doing Teshuva and Moving Closer to G-d

As I increased my knowledge of G–d and His ways,
I wanted to move closer to Him. *Teshuva* means
returning or turning toward G–d and His ways by
learning His will and doing His will. Doing *teshuva*
means choosing to do what G–d wants. We can follow
commandments, such as keeping Shabbat and honor–
ing our parents. We can emulate His ways and act with
kindness and mercy. Consciously doing what G–d
commands makes us more conscious of G–d's pres–
ence in our lives. Rambam tells us that *teshuva* will
bring us closer to G–d and connect us to Him.

Teshuva is great for it brings us closer to the
Divine Presence. *Teshuva*, Rambam says, brings near
those who are far away. When I recognize G–d in the
world, I am closer or more connected to Him. I am
closer to G–d when I turn to Him in times of need.
When I attach myself to His will, I connect myself to
His wisdom.

Looking at a tree, I can see just the tree, or I can
look at the same tree and think about how G–d made
trees out of His kindness to us. We can eat the fruit
and get shade from the leaves. The trunk can be used
for building or the bark for medicine. When I get sick,

I can look to the doctor to heal me or I can look to G-d to heal me. If I perceive G-d as the Healer, then the doctor becomes an instrument of G-d's will. When I am hungry, I can quickly eat my food or I can first stop to say a blessing. If I say the blessing, I am recognizing G-d as the source of my sustenance.

Through *teshuva*, Rambam says, we can draw closer to G-d. In fact, *teshuva* can bring us so close to G-d that He sometimes will answer our cries or prayers immediately, as soon as we ask.

As Rambam says, "And you that connect to the Lord, your G-d, cry out (pray) and you are answered immediately" (*Mishne Torah*, Sefer Hamadah, Hilchot Teshuva 7:7).

I discovered that as I have turned to a more Torah-based life, I have seen some of my prayers answered. My health has improved. I am less angry. I found a job that I wanted. There is more clarity in my decisions about my daughter's future. My relationship with my husband is better. Writing this book has improved my understanding of G-d. As I continue to pray, I hope to receive more guidance.

By doing the mitzvot of the Torah, I am following G-d's will and connecting myself to His wisdom. Following His laws also leads to increased knowledge of G-d and the world. This knowledge will lead to love of G-d which results in happiness and life in this world and in the World to Come.

Again Rambam explains this perfectly, "When

we fulfill all the mitzvot of the Torah, all the good things of this world will come to us...We will not be busy all our days with matters pertaining to our bodily needs, but will have leisure to learn wisdom and do commandments, in order to attain life in the World to Come. 'And it will be our righteous duty, that we do all these commandments before the Lord, our G–d, as He has commanded us' (Deuteronomy 6:25). If you have served G–d with joy and followed His way, He will give to you those blessings and avert from you those curses, so that you will have leisure to become wise in the Torah...so you will enjoy both worlds—a happy life in this earthly world leading to the life in the World to Come" (*Mishne Torah*, Sefer Hamadah, Hilchot Teshuva 9:1).

G–d will protect us if we do His will. G–d will make it possible for us to continue learning and doing His mitzvot. We will find ourselves with the time and means to continue following His ways.

It is tempting to think that I will have wealth and pleasure if I follow all of the commandments. This is *not* the promise. The major reward for doing G–d's will is in the World to Come. The promise is that I will get what I need in this world so that I will have time to learn and become wise in the Torah. The wisdom that I gain will allow me to enjoy this life by teaching me to be satisfied with what I have. G–d will give me what I need, not necessarily what I want or think I need.

Following the Commandments

The Torah gives us many commandments to follow G-d's will. There are commandments for all areas of our lives—what to eat, how to dress, how to observe Shabbat, and how to relate to other people. The commandments are G-d's instructions for life. We can and should enjoy the pleasures of life as gifts from G-d as long as we follow His guidelines.

If done with the proper intent, the Torah's laws and mitzvot can lead us to an increased love and knowledge of G-d. As we make good choices, we make room for G-d in our lives. When I follow G-d's commandments, with the intent to do the right thing and come closer to Him, I increase my love and knowledge of G-d.

Rambam tells us that when we come to love G-d, we begin to strive for knowledge for the sake of knowledge. We do what is right because it is right. We serve G-d and benefit ourselves with happiness that results from our striving to know Him.

Rambam also notes that we should strive to serve G-d out of love and occupy oneself with Torah and commandments, and walk in the paths of wisdom, *not* because of concerns of this world, the fear of punishment or the hope of receiving benefits but simply because we believe it is the truth. In the end, goodness will come as the result of what one does (*Mishne Torah*, Sefer Hamadah, Hilchot Teshuva 10:2).

Love of G–d comes from knowledge of G–d and His ways and leads to a desire to learn more. More knowledge leads to more love. More love leads to a desire for more knowledge. Rambam describes a love of G–d that is intense and all consuming.

What is the appropriate love of G–d? Rambam says it is to love G–d with a great and exceeding love, a love that is so strong that one's soul is bound with this love. We should always be contemplating it, like someone who is love–sick, whose mind is never free from his or her passion for someone. The thought of this person fills their heart at all times, when sitting down or rising up, when eating or drinking. The love of G–d should be even more intense for those who love Him. And this love should continually possess them, even as He commanded us in Deuteronomy 6:5, "with all your heart and with all your soul" (*Mishne Torah*, Sefer Hamadah, Hilchot Teshuva 10:3).

A wonderful line in Psalms sums up this love— "Happy is the man who fears the Lord, who delights greatly in His commandments" (Psalms 112:1).

Choosing a Meaningful Life

I am not on such a high level of love that I spend all day contemplating G–d. Nor have I given up every- thing else in the world. However, even my small striv- ing to know more has made me a more satisfied and happier person. Learning has led me to strive for more knowledge of G–d. This has led me to a happier life. Following G–d's commandments has not led to a pain-less life of economic wealth and pleasure. My happi-ness is inward and has resulted because I've gotten closer to G–d and His ways even while experiencing the normal pain and difficulty that exist in life.

Since I have begun learning Torah, I have begun to make more choices in how I relate to others, and I can see my choices with more clarity. I have better guidelines to discern which actions are healthier. An animal makes no conscious choices. It follows its instincts. My conscious choices make me human. My conscious choices have brought me to try and build a connection with G–d.

Rambam does not ask us to "believe" in G–d's existence. He tells us to "know" that G–d exists. Our belief in G–d, as Jews, is based on knowledge of G–d and His will, which we can develop intellectually by study and experientially in the world. Rambam explains that it is obligatory for each and every one of us to attempt to gain greater knowledge of G–d to the utmost of our capacity, until we personally come to know Him.

Since it is impossible to actually know G–d as He is, the expression "knowing G–d" refers to knowing His ways and His world leading to love and fear of Him. In Sefer Hamadah (introduction to chapter 1), Rambam tells us that the first commandment of the Ten Commandments: "You shall love the Lord your

G-d" is the first of the ten precepts in the laws concerning the basic principles of the Torah. Loving G-d
and fearing Him are the fifth and sixth principles.

For all my acquired knowledge, I know it's impossible to learn the truth or essence of G-d's existence. I
have a lifetime to learn what I am capable of learning.
For now, I have uncovered my essence as a spiritual,
knowing human being. I know the direction of my life
is my choice and I am on the road to building a
healthy lifestyle. For me this means choosing to be less
angry, judgmental, and controlling. It means being
more satisfied with what I have as I try to walk in
G-d's ways.

Although I made the choice to know G-d better
and to do His will, I could not do it by myself.
Learning and intent are essential, but they were not
enough for me. Knowledge must lead to action and
change. I needed a way to put this knowledge of what
is right into my daily life. This was impossible for me
to do by myself, even with the help of many books.

I've given here only a brief accounting of some of
the basic Torah principles. It is important to build an
understanding that G-d created us with the purpose
to come to know His ways, with an increased love and
fear of Him. It is essential to know that we were given
the ability to make free-will moral choices. We can
also make the choice to improve ourselves and connect ourselves to G-d's will. Making the right choices
will make us healthier and happier. How to make

those choices and institute changes in ourselves is a difficult task. A strong understanding of basic Torah principles combined with the Twelve Steps creates a powerful combination for change.

G–d did not create humans to be alone and self–sufficient. He wants us to turn to others and to turn to Him. I pray to G–d for His guidance and assistance. I attend lectures and learn with other people. Through the Twelve Steps which I follow, I am learning to seek help from others and from G–d. Step by step, I am learning what it means to make healthy choices and live as a conscious, thinking, spiritual human being. The Twelve Steps help me make good choices in a Torah framework, one step at a time.

The Twelve Steps combined with Torah is very powerful—you may find in reading this any precon-ceived notions you have could be forever changed. You may find the strength that you need to begin starting over, one step at a time.

Step One

We admitted that we were powerless over our own urges, and that our lives had become unmanageable.

✦ ✦ ✦

Feeling Hopeless
and Out of Control

Here we begin the Twelve Steps as adapted within a Torah framework.

Step One

We admitted that we were powerless over our own urges, and that our lives had become unmanageable.

In Step One, we acknowledge our inability or our difficulty coping with and controlling the circumstances of our lives. This idea is actually very Jewish. We can find references to this in Psalms:

"Man is like a breath. His days are like a passing shadow" (Psalms 144:4).

"Do not rely on nobles, nor on a human being who has no power of deliverance. When his spirit departs, he returns to his earth. On that day his plans all perish" (Psalms 146:3–4).

An alcoholic admits that he or she has no power over alcohol. An overeater admits that he or she has no power over food. The codependent admits that he or she has no power over their urges to control and perfect other people. We all have aspects of our lives over which we have no power. For some of us it may be alcohol, drugs, food, or the urge to make people better. For others it may be emotional tendencies, such as rage or depression. It may be the urge to react from instinct rather than to act after careful deliberation.

Of course, we recognize that we have very limited control over things like intelligence, physical makeup, predispositions, and health. Whether we want to or not, we will get hungry, thirsty, and tired. Our physical bodies will break down. Science and medicine have made wonderful strides, but no one lives forever.

My life had become unmanageable when I tried to exercise power and control over things that were not in my power to control. I had been living with a distorted perception of reality. I had internalized the fantasy that people have unlimited power. My dream was that I could do anything I set my mind and body to do, if only I tried hard enough.

After completing college and getting my teacher's license, I thought that I would be able to get any job I wanted, if I sent out enough applications, and that I would be promoted and financially rewarded, as long as I worked effectively. I assumed that I would easily find a husband and have as many children as I wanted whenever I desired. Good health was something I took for granted, as long as I was reasonably careful about food, sleep and exercise.

This was all fantasy. I couldn't find any good teaching jobs. Nobody in the administration of the schools I taught in seemed to care how effective I was as a teacher. My husband and I had only one child, and no matter how careful I was, I had problems with my health. The reality was that there were many things over which I had no power—or very limited power—to change, control, or even influence. No matter how hard I tried, I often found that I could not even modify or perfect myself, never mind other people or events external to myself. The world continued to bombard me with events that were beyond my control. Trying to maintain power and control led to frustration, immobilization, anxiety, fatigue, and illness.

Once I realized there is one Power in the world and that Power is G–d, not me, a great weight was lifted off my shoulders. When I believe that I should control, alter, change, modify, or perfect other people or events, I am believing in myself as a power that stands apart from the ultimate Power. By so doing, I make myself into a god. This is idolatry.

I have learned that any power or strength I do have has been given to me by G–d. I am an instrument of G–d's will. There is no power separate from G–d. I can make G–d my partner, but it is He Who will determine if I am successful.

Admitting Our Powerlessness

This first step of admitting my powerlessness became my key to making the idea of G–d as the only Power a reality. This concept became a part of my life, a part of my very being. When I began to let go of what I discovered to be a codependent's need to have power and control over other people, I began real *teshuva* or change. I gave up the idolatrous notion that I had godlike power and faced life as a person who has chosen to live by the will of G–d.

It is no coincidence that admitting our powerlessness is the first step of recovery, as well as the first step toward *teshuva* and G–d. It is also no coincidence that the first of the Ten Commandments is the belief in the one and only unlimited Power: "I am Hashem, your G–d, Who brought you out of the land of Egypt, out of the house of bondage" (Exod.20:2). The second commandment is a prohibition against idolatry: "You shall not have any other gods before Me" (Exod. 20:3).

This is also Rambam's first principle stated in the *Mishne Torah*: "The basic principle of all basic principles and the pillar of all sciences is to realize that there is a First Being who brought every thing that exists into being" (*Mishne Torah*, Sefer Hamadah, Hilchot Yesodei HaTorah 1:1). The Twelve Steps and the Torah, it seems, begin with the same premise—there is only one power and this power is G–d.

Every day I pray and recite the Shema prayer,

declaring and reminding myself that G–d is One. G–d is the ultimate unlimited Power. Admitting my power-lessness always makes me feel a little small. I suppose that is what humility is all about. However, I have dis-covered that there are many positives to letting go of control. It means that I can let go of judging another or myself when I realize how limited we all are. It means that I can accept imperfection in myself and others. Letting go of trying to maintain the impossible allows me to focus on what I *can* do and on what I need. It creates the possibility of looking outside of myself for help. This means taking an active role in becoming healthy, both physically and spiritually. I can work toward taking mental charge of my life by making better choices in what I do and in how I relate to other people. I consult with rabbis, teachers, and friends. I pray.

Making Free Will Choices

We all have free will to make choices. However, I do not have power over what will happen as a result of those choices. Just because I decide to do some-thing does *not* insure that it will happen. People or events can easily change the direction of my inten-tions. Although I cannot control the outcome of those choices, I do have the ability to control any thoughts and reactions to what happens. I can choose to be calm or angry. I can choose to give up or I can choose to try again.

I have chosen to try and act according to the ways of Torah, rather than simply following my physical instincts. I try to keep the idea of my powerlessness in mind. When I give charity or when I do good deeds for people, I try to help them instead of crossing the boundary between helping and interfering with their free will and the choices they may make to take care of themselves.

I started to step back from my codependent need of always being in charge. This was possible by making a conscious attempt *not* to control everything and everyone. I had to learn to accept other people's right to control their own lives, to make their own plans and decisions—whether the results were good or bad. Sometimes if I let go, I am pleasantly surprised. Recently, I was away from home for two days. When I returned, my daughter informed me that she had made my bed, cleaned up the living room, put away the dishes, and mopped the floor. On the other hand, the surprises are not always pleasant. Sometimes I let go and do not like what happens. Very often, I return home and find the house a mess. I had to learn to accept other people's right to make what I may consider bad choices. It is also important to accept my right to make a mistake.

This step has not been easy for me. For all my life, I believed that it was my job to take care of things, to fix things, to control people and events, and to make everything perfect. If my family went on a vacation and not everyone was happy, I felt it was my fault for not planning better.

When my daughter was an infant, I hated to hear her cry. So, I held her closely, knowing that if she would keep still for only a minute, she would fall asleep. When she was tired and cranky, I blamed myself for not making sure that she got to bed on time. When she went off to school, it was my job to get her out to the bus on schedule. I often spent the whole morning yelling at her to hurry up. The more I yelled, the slower she moved.

I took responsibility for my husband's life also. I felt it was my fault if he was unhappy. When my mother was diagnosed with cancer, I made it my job to try to find alternative doctors and medicine, often spending hours on the phone trying to make arrangements. When my father temporarily moved into our house, I took responsibility for him also. Not only did I make arrangements for his doctors and therapists, I had to be home to make his breakfast, lunch and dinner.

I was so busy taking care of everyone else that I became immobilized when it came to taking care of myself. It became impossible to leave my house because there was no time and too much to do. I put off seeing a gastroenterologist for myself, although I suffered from attacks of pain that sometimes lasted from six to ten hours. There was no way to go to my study class at night, because either my husband needed me to work with him or my daughter needed me to help her go to sleep.

Who assigned me this tremendous job? Who de-
manded such devotion? Only I. Nobody else.

Choosing to Be Free

I was introduced to the idea of codependency and
the Twelve Steps of recovery exactly at the time that I
most needed them. The Twelve Steps were discussed by
my Torah study group. We began to see the relationship between the steps and Torah. I continued to talk
to my teachers, Dr. Blema Feinstein and Rabbi Jonathan
Sacks. They always helped to clarify my thinking.

Slowly, but surely, I began to free myself as I had
enslaved myself. I announced to my daughter that I
was giving up my job as head nag. The first day she
rushed out to the bus without brushing her hair and
teeth and without eating her breakfast. This rushing
does not happen too often anymore, and she only
missed a bus once. I stopped checking up on her and
questioning her in the morning. Now I rarely see her
without a hairbrush, and if she is running late, she
grabs a piece of fruit on the way out. Letting go gives
everyone back their dignity and their right to be
themselves.

It is not my job to help anyone to be perfect
according to my recipe! I had somehow stepped over
the boundary between being a caring person and trying to control and wield power over others. Once I
gave that power back to the ultimate Source of power,

I could appreciate people and life much more.

Now I can try to guide my daughter in decisions, such as leisure activities and appropriate behavior, without feeling like a failure myself if she makes bad choices. My self-esteem does not have to fall just because my husband does something that I feel is wrong. I can offer suggestions when I sense that they will be followed and hold back my ideas when I sense that they cannot be heard. Most people are pretty capable and can take care of themselves without my interference.

I am learning to be accepting when things are not done my way. The outcome may not always please me. That is also okay. Living in the present, I am trying to accept every moment and each person as precious.

To review the First Step: We admit that we are powerless over our own urges and that our lives have become unmanageable. We may think we can control our intake of alcohol, food, drugs, or our control of other people, or our own passions. We must recognize the difference between what we can control and what we cannot. We must recognize the price we pay physically, emotionally, and spiritually for trying to maintain control.

Give up the attempt to be all powerful and start to live as a thinking, spiritual human being. Become empowered by letting go. It is a difficult and important step, but it is worth the effort. It is the first step toward a happier life.

Step Two

Came to believe that a Power greater than ourselves could restore us to sanity.

✦ ✦ ✦

Letting Go and Accepting G-d

In Step One, we learned that we alone do not control the vagaries of our lives and that we have no right to control the lives of others. Within the Torah framework, we acknowledge G–d's ultimate Power. We will explore G–d's Power further in this chapter.

Step Two

Came to believe that a Power greater than ourselves could restore us to sanity.

References to letting go and accepting G–d are plentiful in the Torah. In Exodus we find the verse: "Who is like You among the heavenly powers. Who is like You, mighty in holiness, too awesome for praise" (15:11). In Psalms it says: "Cast your burden upon G–d and He will sustain you" (55:23).

In Step One, I acknowledged that I am lacking in power and that my actions can be harmful to my well being. In so doing, I recognized that there is an ultimate Power, much greater than I. Step Two reminds me that after I've released control to a Power greater than I, this Power can restore me to a healthier and happier life.

Rambam explains how G–d is our Creator, and we can place our troubles with G–d and rely on His help. As it states in *Shema* in the daily prayers, "Hear, O Israel, Hashem is our G–d, Hashem is One." (The Creator and Sustainer are One.)

Rambam explains that since G–d is the Power Who created us, He is also the Power Who can help us. Nothing can exist without G–d's support. Rambam tells us that "all existing things exist only through His true existence. If it could be imagined that G–d did not exist, nothing else could possibly exist. Everyone is in need of G–d, the G–d of the universe, the Lord of all the earth. G–d controls the sphere of the universe with a power that has no end or limit. The sphere is always revolving and it is G–d, blessed be He, who without hand or body, causes it to revolve" (*Mishne Torah*, Sefer Hamadah, Hilchot Yesodei HaTorah 1:5).

If we look at the history of the Jews we see that the Israelites were slaves in Egypt. After more than two hundred years of suffering, G–d sent Moshe to bring out His people. But after meeting with Moshe, Pharaoh increased the people's burden. The Israelites complained bitterly to Moshe and Aaron:

"…and they said to them: 'May G–d look down

upon you and judge, because you have brought us into foul odor in the eyes of Pharaoh and his servants.' Moshe returned to G-d and said, 'My Lord! For what purpose have You made misfortune the lot of this people? Why did You send me? And ever since I came to Pharaoh to speak in Your Name, he has abused the people even more, and You have not rescued Your people even from this?' And G-d said to Moshe: 'Now you will see what I will do to Pharaoh, for by a strong hand will he let them go'" (Exodus 5:21–6:1).

G-d revealed a name to Moshe that no one had previously known, the ineffable Name, the Tetragrammaton: G-d spoke to Moshe and said to him, "I am Hashem" (Exodus 6:2).

In doing this, Rabbi Samson Raphael Hirsch explains, G-d revealed His aspect of sovereignty and control in this name. The name means He was, He is, and He will always be. G-d is timeless. Not only is He the hidden Creator, but He is presently creating and will continue to do so forever. He sustains the world and everything in it at every moment.

Rabbi Samson Raphael Hirsch explains, in his commentary on this verse, that we are not victims of situations that are already in existence. The natural result of living in Egypt would have been the destruction of the Jewish people. Our survival, despite our many weaknesses, indicates that G-d controls and directs all of reality. Until now, Hirsch says, all the

despair, the insults, the misery and the distress had
developed from natural circumstances that G–d per-
mitted to develop. These had been the natural results
of Egypt's corruption and might against Israel's weak-
ness and helplessness. But now "I am Hashem Who
brings new things into being: I am the One Who
exercises His will independently of and despite existing realities."

Through the redemption of Israel, G–d showed
Israel and the world that His control is above and
beyond nature. G–d can change the natural course of
events. Nature's control is an illusion, a deception that
needs to be exposed in order to see G–d as the true
cause of reality.

G–d wants us to turn to Him. The world is set up
so that we will falter. Struggling and failing causes us
to seek G–d's help. When I began studying Torah, Dr.
Blema Feinstein advised me to turn to G–d with
gratitude when things are going well. When we do
not turn to G–d voluntarily, the events of life will
force us to turn to Him when we desperately need
His help.

Despair is often the result of faulty judgment and
bad choices. One wrong decision easily leads to another. Harmful habits develop, and we lose the man-
agement and the sanity of our lives. We could be
experiencing what Rambam calls "an illness of the
soul." The greatest harm occurs when we act in a
destructive way and harm ourselves, and our connec-

tion to G-d, since building a connection to G-d is our purpose in life.

For me, I sought change and help when I realized my soul was sick. I was feeling angry, anxious, tired and frustrated. How could I enjoy any good in life? Daily existence became increasingly burdensome as I, in my codependent way, took on more and more responsibility for other people's happiness.

It was time to change, but I could not do it alone. I was powerless. I wanted to heal my soul and my body, so I studied and travelled to lectures and meetings. Finally, I realized that only G-d could help me, because only G-d has the power to control, alter, modify, and affect people and events. He had to be my partner. My success would be in G-d's hands. I prayed for His help.

In Biblical times, when Jewish soldiers went to battle, they prayed for Divine assistance. The Torah teaches us that when these soldiers went to battle without G-d's help, they were not successful.

We are also in a battle, a constant battle for our lives. We're just not aware of this. Without G-d's help we cannot succeed. Our society's values are distorted, and many forces work hard to make us fail. Many of our plans will be thwarted. Our bodies will eventually break down. Physical nature pulls us to strive for comfort, instead of to attempt to find truth and knowledge of G-d. Step Two helps us understand that only a Power greater than ourselves can restore us to a more sane existence. Only G-d can restore us to health and happiness.

Step Three

Made a decision to turn our will and our lives over to the care of G-d, as we understood G-d.

✦ ✦ ✦

Doing G-d's Will

In Step Two, we acknowledged that the only One Who can restore us to health, both spiritually and physically is G-d. In Step Three, we make the commitment to entrust our souls and our bodies to G-d's Power.

Step Three

Made a decision to turn our will and our lives over to the care of G-d, as we understood G-d.

Pirke Avot (Ethics of the Fathers) states: "Do His will as you would do your own will, so that He may do your will just as He does His will. Set aside your will for the sake of His will, so that He may set aside the will of others before your will" (Rabban Gamliel, *Pirke Avot*, 2:4).

Step Three is about accepting and submitting to

G-d's will. Once we recognize our limitations, we can begin to forgive ourselves for our failings, and pray to G-d for help. We can stop trying to enforce our will and turn our will over to Him. Acknowledging that we are not the masters of our lives, we turn our lives over to the true Master. Happiness will occur when we become satisfied with what G-d gives us. In the Twelve Step program we say, "Let go and let G-d." When we let go, we make space for G-d to do His will.

In the classical Twelve Steps, G-d is not defined, since the original writers of the Twelve Steps did not want to discourage or exclude anyone because of their particular belief or lack of belief. So, He is "G-d, as we understand G-d." Turning our will and lives over to the care of a higher Power of the universe is healthy, even when the Power is undefined. It helps people to recover. Turning our will and our lives over to the care of G-d is good for our mental and physical health.

The Torah defines the higher Power as G-d. And the Torah explains that our very purpose in this world is to come to know G-d and to do His will. We accept what happens to us in life as G-d's will. We try to grow as healthy human beings, learning from all our experiences.

When I am up against a seemingly impossible situation, I always remind myself: This is G-d's will so I make it my will. When I feel upset and disappointed, I remind myself: This is G-d's will and I can make it my will. I *can* depend on G-d. G-d created the world to benefit me. His will is good for me, even if I may be in pain at that moment. I pray for G-d's help so that I can be satisfied with what He gives me.

Alcoholics believe they are in control and can have one drink without wanting another. Overeaters are sure that just one more cookie would be okay. Codependents try to change one more person in just one area of life. We think that we can control our urges but we must admit that often we cannot.

In Step Three—we stop trying to force our own will and control over life. We let go and give that job back to G-d. We let G-d's will reign in the world. We replace guilt with gratitude. No doubt, we have had problems and failings, but we are thankful anyway, because we were given the gift of life and because it all is part of G-d's will. G-d brought us to this place so that we can learn how to *live* life instead of simply survive it.

For example, I have accepted that I tend to take charge of everyone. Thankfully, this tendency brought me to the Twelve Steps. I have begun to change my controlling nature and check my anger. Other people have shown me how to relate to G-d on a more personal level.

Now, I do not always have to be in charge or impose my opinion about how things should be. Sometimes, I can even sit back and observe. For instance, I have learned to accept that my husband and daughter take a longer time to get ready than I when we are going out. Instead of rushing my family, getting angry or anxious, I sit down and read a book. The world does not stop turning when we are late. Most of the time, it makes absolutely no difference. In fact, sometimes, not being exactly on time has turned out to our advantage. I learned to be more patient when I began to accept my husband's and daughter's lateness. To be sure, I don't believe I should set out to be late, nor carry it to excess, but neither do I need to be a slave to time.

Acceptance does not mean that we must accept undesirable events or situations that occur to us. Jewish law not only allows us to be active but encourages us to act. We are never supposed to prolong a situation where anyone is being harmed, including ourselves. The Biblical commandment of saving a life takes precedence over other commandments. We must, of course, take care of ourselves—removing ourselves from abusive situations and visiting doctors when we are ill. We struggle against things that go wrong in our lives and seek out Torah scholars and good friends. We focus on solutions when it is possible and accept only things that cannot be changed. Then we can attempt to be satisfied with what we have.

Defining G-d's Will

I often struggle trying to determine what is G-d's will. There are three ways that help me acquire that knowledge. I observe His world, I study His words, and I pray.

Learning Torah has taught me that whatever happens is G-d's will and is ultimately for the good. Both my successful and unsuccessful endeavors serve G-d's purpose and ultimately benefit me. G-d guides all of reality including the events of my life. Somehow in His Divine plan of life, I receive what I need in order to grow as a human being and sometimes some of my prayers are answered.

It is often difficult to see the good in extremely tragic and painful events. It is helpful to begin to see good in the smaller events of life. Experiencing the goodness of mundane events opens the possibility that good is there even when it is not apparent.

Someone recently stepped on something that was directly over my toe. It was extremely painful and I sat down on my bed. From that vantage point, I noticed a nail sticking out of the wall. Concerned that someone could get hurt, I went to the kitchen for a hammer. While I was in the kitchen I noticed some food that I had forgotten to put away. Since I had been getting ready to go to sleep, the food would have remained out all night and spoiled. My hurt toe saved my food and protected my family from being harmed by the nail. What seemed like a negative turned out to be a positive. I had experienced G-d's goodness and guidance. *Gam zu l'tova*—this is also for the good.

I have found it easier now to see the good in tragedies that do not affect me directly. I hear about disasters in the news, and I am always impressed by the help and concern of people. Whether it is a hurricane, earthquake, or bombing, people rush to help with supplies, money, and manpower. I have opened my eyes to see the positives. I know that there are many kind and generous people in the world, even though they may not be obvious in our daily life.

As we observe the goodness in our lives and in the world, we can come to love G–d and serve Him with love by accepting and following His will. As Rambam tells us:

"When we fulfill all the *mitzvot* of the Torah, all the good things of this world will come to us" (*Mishne Torah*, Sefer Hamadah, Hilchot Teshuva 9:1).

Pain and Suffering

Personal suffering is probably the most difficult thing to accept as G–d's will. Sometimes things will happen that we will be unable to understand or to accept. The Torah tells us that G–d is all knowing, all powerful, and all good. Even suffering is part of G–d's will. Suffering is often necessary for our growth as thinking human beings. Growth assists us in not acting automatically.

If the purpose of life is to acquire material possessions, power, money, or physical pleasure or comfort, then any loss will be bad. By contrast, if the purpose of life is to become a thinking/spiritual person, then loss can signify opportunity. Loss becomes an avenue for growth, for growing closer to people and G-d. As we gain an understanding of people, the world, and G-d's ways, we will ultimately lead a happier life.

It is true that I cannot know exactly why things happen to me. However, I can still choose how I will respond to harmful or unhappy situations. All pain and suffering is a signal that I need to turn to G-d.

Minor problems are easier to comprehend. Pain over minor discomforts in life is a sign that we have distorted our priorities about what is important and necessary.

The rabbis of the Talmud say that even when you feel minor discomfort, such as when you reach into your pocket for change and choose the wrong coin, even this momentary inconvenience can remind you to reevaluate yourself, your relationships to people and your knowledge and connection to G-d and to recognize what is important in life. This is not a time to blame G-d or yourself. In turning your will over to G-d, every event becomes an opportunity to grow.

I recall one evening while I waited for a car ride to the train. I realized that I had missed the first train and, if my car ride didn't arrive soon, I might miss the second. I checked my anger and anxiety. I told myself that this, too, was G-d's will. Perhaps I needed more practice at being patient and giving the other person the benefit of the doubt. Perhaps missing the train enabled me to avoid some unforeseen disaster. I wait-ed calmly for a half hour. My ride came, and I made the second train by two minutes. Focussing on my will to make an early train only made me angry. By remembering that whatever happens to me is G–d's will, I was able to accept the situation and substitute serenity for needless tension.

Acceptance of a seemingly bad situation, which I certainly would not choose, allows me to use the time as an opportunity to improve my character traits and draw closer to G–d. In this way, I can experience the goodness of G–d's will in the world, at each moment in my life, the moments I like, as well as the moments I do not like. If I read through the Torah, I can gain an understanding of the value of following G–d's will as demonstrated in the past.

Studying His Words

Review the historical examples in the Torah and you'll see that goodness, success and life, for both individuals and for the Jewish nation as a whole was always a result of following G–d's will. Failure of people's plans, and sometimes death for various individuals, was often the consequence of going against His will.

Abraham merited having the Jewish nation descend from him because he adopted G–d's will to such an extent that he was willing to sacrifice his own son if that's what G–d asked. In Queen Esther's merit, the Jewish people were saved from the wickedness of Haman. She followed G–d's will, even though it meant living a life that she would never have chosen for herself. King Saul lost his life, and the kingship of Israel was lost to his descendants, because he did what he thought was right, even though G-d had instructed him otherwise.

The Jewish people have survived and prospered for thousands of years on the certainty of the Torah's guidance. Our ancient training in the ways of Torah has sustained us. We have inherited the spiritual work of our ancestors. The characteristics that they personally developed became intrinsic to the Jewish people. Many stories are told of Jews who sacrificed their lives to be Jews, including many of these people who had never consciously learned or observed the Torah's commandments. Such sacrifice itself is part of the Torah's teaching.

Studying G-d's words by learning Torah gives us insight into G-d's will for our world. We can act according to G-d's will by following His commandments and laws. The Hebrew word, *halacha*, means law and is derived from the same root in Hebrew as the word, *walk*. As it says in Deuteronomy 28:9: "G-d will raise you up for Himself to be a holy people as He swore to you if you keep the commandments and walk in His ways ."

As Jews, we are all obligated to learn what we need to know in order to serve G-d. Men have the additional obligation of learning for the sake of learning, whether or not there are apparent practical applications.

Rambam tells us: "Every Israelite is under obligation to study Torah, whether poor or rich, in sound
health or ailing, in the vigor of youth or very old and
feeble" (*Mishne Torah*, Sefer Hamadah, Hilchot Talmud Torah 1:8).

Until what period in life ought one study Torah?
Until the day of one's death as it is said, "and that they
(the precepts) not depart from your heart" (*Mishne
Torah*, Sefer Hamadah, Hilchot Talmud Torah 1:10).

There is an enormous amount of knowledge available for learning G–d's ways, His *halacha*. I have tried
not to be discouraged. Even the small amount that I
have learned has helped me to clarify His will. Following the commandments has helped to improve my
character by shifting my focus away from the pursuit
of physical comfort.

I eat kosher food. I have trained myself to eat only
what G–d tells me to through the laws of the Torah. I
have learned to pay less attention to my physical
urges in favor of following G–d's will. Even my daughter will forgo a piece of candy when she is told that it
is not kosher.

Following the laws of Shabbat has also pulled me
away from material existence in favor of a spiritual
connection to G–d. For one day each week, I stop trying to master the world. Instead, I acknowledge its one
true Master.

Late one Friday afternoon, I was preparing a

noodle pooding, when I noticed a small bug floating in the noodle pot. The bug may have caused the noodles to be unkosher. If they were still kosher, it was wasteful to throw them away. I removed the bug and not sure what to do, I called my rabbi, but his line was busy. Glancing at the clock, I noted that there would not be enough time to drive to his house and back for the answer and still bake the noodle pudding before the beginning of Shabbat. I called another rabbi. After asking about the size and condition of the bug, he said that he would have to look up the matter and would call me back. He called back a few minutes later to say that the noodles were kosher. It would have been easier to throw out the noodles and forget about it. I was more concerned about doing what was right. I have gotten used to bending my will for the sake of following G-d's laws.

The commandments and laws of the Torah serve G-d's purpose and benefit me. Doing mitzvot has helped me grow. Following commandments and laws trains me to turn my will and life over to the care of G-d.

I have benefited from following G-d's commandments and laws because accepting and doing G-d's will keeps me healthy and allows me to live a full life instead of merely surviving. I am less angry and anxious because I have learned to accept life's events as G-d's will. I am less frustrated and unhappy because I consider doing G-d's will more important than mate-

rial accomplishments. Following G–d's commandments has not kept unhappy events out of my life.
Instead it has helped me to become a healthier and
happier person, in spite of life's pain and disappoint-
ment.

Praying for Help

There are many times when I am still at a loss at
what to do. So, I let go and pray to G–d for a solution.
I became an observant Jew in 1989. I tried to follow
G–d's commandments to the best of my ability. When
I felt troubled, I would try to find my own solutions. I
thought and read books and tried to analyze my situation. By working the Twelve Steps and talking to others, I finally came to the realization that I also could
personally ask for G–d's help.

I decided that my daughter needed to be in a different Jewish Day School. There were two other alter-
natives. Only one was Orthodox. I thought that the
Orthodox Yeshiva would be the better choice based
on our lifestyle, but I was not really sure. The other
school had a big field, playground, and gym. It had a
great lunch program, and offered art and music. I was
so troubled by this decision that I found myself in
tears. I called out to G–d for help, admitting that I did
not know what to do. My mind was not clear—I was
confused.

One hour later a friend called me. Her daughter
was attending the non–Orthodox school. She told me

a few things about the school that bothered me, and I relayed this information to my husband. We decided the Orthodox school was more appropriate for our needs.

I think that intense personal prayer clears the mind so that we can judge information more clearly. Praying opened me to G–d's guidance and suddenly, the right decision was clear.

Seeking G-d's Will

When you face events in life that you do not like or do not want to deal with, I have observed that you have three choices. This is true whether they are serious, like death in the family, or merely annoying, like your spouse leaving dirty socks on the floor. When you face commandments or laws that are difficult and demanding, you have the same choices. You can choose anger, distraction, or acceptance.

Giving in to anger and bitterness would be rejecting G–d. By distracting yourself with physical pleasures, you could try to ignore the whole issue (also rejecting G–d's guidance). The pleasures of going to the movies or of having another piece of cake or another drink can be very effective distractions. You can try to make the choice to accept and submit yourself to G–d's will, growing and becoming healthier both mentally and physically. You can try to accept as G–d's will what cannot be changed and use it as an opportunity to move toward Him.

When I do not accept G–d's will, I become blind to reality and unable to see the truth. I become a slave to my physical urges and distortions of how I think things should be. Blinded to the truth of G–d's wisdom, I try to force my own distorted view of reality. I stop seeing the value in others because they are not acting as I think they should. I denigrate others because I feel that I could do a better job. I even denigrate myself because I think that I should have done a better job.

For many years after I graduated college I tried to get a public school teaching job. Since there were very few jobs available in my area and an abundance of teachers applying for them, I took low paying private school jobs and each year continued to search for a better job. I expended an enormous amount of time, energy, and resources, because I thought that I should be able to get a good teaching job. I built up strong negative feelings for all of those teachers and principals who had somehow made it into the system. The notion that perhaps I didn't try hard enough kept creeping into my thoughts. When I finally woke up to the reality of the employment situation in the community where I live on Long Island, I realized that I needed to do something else. I prayed to G–d for help, took a different direction, and now I work as a Recreational Therapist at the Long Island State Veteran's Home.

Ignoring the obvious makes it possible to believe

that a human knows better than G-d what is right. In the Torah we find that G-d chose Moshe and Aaron to lead the Jewish people out of Egypt. Korach could not accept this. He thought that he should be the leader. He challenged their authority. He was blinded by how he thought things should be. Consequently, he and his followers were swallowed by the earth.

When you set aside G-d's will in favor of your own, you set yourself up for failure. Think of what Moshe said to the Israelites when they decided to go into battle for the land after G-d had prohibited it.

"Why do you now transgress the command of G-d? This will not succeed" (Numbers 14:41).

Even our failures serve G-d's will. They serve as avenues for growth. The Jewish people were ordered to wander in the desert for forty years after they had refused to go into the land as commanded by G-d. Those years of isolation forged them into a strong nation that has survived for thousands of years.

We can learn and grow from every single thing that happens to us and from everyone we meet. This is possible when we turn our will and our life over to G-d's care. When we study His words of Torah, we gain a clearer vision of His will. When we accept events as His will, we can see life more clearly. By not trying to enforce our distortions of reality, we can refrain from blinding ourselves to obvious truths. If we truly comprehended that only G-d is all powerful, knowing and good, then we would never attempt to

control other people or events but accept the imperfections in life. If we clearly understood that everything comes from G-d, how could we be greedy, arrogant, or jealous? Instead, we would humbly seek to do
G-d's will. Being satisfied with what He gives us makes
us happier. Turning our will over to the care of G-d
will give us a better life.

Step Four

Made a searching and fearless moral inventory of ourselves.

✦ ✦ ✦

Looking Inward

In Step Three, we made a decision to let go of the control we try to impose on ourselves and others and allow G-d to be the Master of our lives. We recognized that this is a healthy thing to do, regardless of how we understand the concept of a higher Power. Now we are ready to begin to explore our inner selves. Step Four entails making a comprehensive moral inventory of ourselves.

Step Four

Made a searching and fearless moral inventory of ourselves.

There are many sources that provide us with guidelines for understanding how to compile this moral inventory. For example, in describing the significance of the sounding of the *shofar* (ram's horn) on Rosh Hashanah, Rambam states:

"Awake, awake, oh sleepers, from your sleep. Oh slumberers, rise from your slumbers, and examine your deeds. Return in *teshuva*, and remember your Creator" (*Mishne Torah*, Sefer Hamadah, Hilchot Teshuva 3:4).

Rambam emphasizes examining one's actions. In his important book, *The Gates of Repentance*, Rabbi Yonah of Gerona tells us to record and review our failings in the observance of the commandments.

He also says that everyone engaged in *teshuva* should keep a written record of the areas in which they have gone astray and of the commandments they have fallen short of fulfilling. These records should then be reviewed daily (*The Gates of Repentance*, 1:8).

Defining the Inventory

What exactly is a searching and fearless moral inventory? What is the point of examining our deeds? When I started to focus on Step Four these were the first questions I needed to consider.

Searching implies taking a look that probes beyond the surface into deep and hidden places. Searching ourselves requires time and energy. Each search can unlock more of the mystery.

"Fearless" implies a lack of fear. I can be fearless only if I am coming from strength, if I feel essentially good about myself. Once you've really worked the first three Steps and once you feel confident to rely on G–d, you will have gained strength. Because you were created by the Eternal Source of goodness in His image you can know that essentially you are good. In *Pirke Avot* (Ethics of the Fathers) it is written that we must not think of ourselves as wicked or evil, even if we do something wrong. Once we view ourselves as wicked, it becomes impossible to change, for, after all, our nature is wicked. The purpose of this personal search is not to condemn ourselves as bad or evil and incapable of change, but to examine our past and what we have been doing. Then we can learn for the future what is good and what is harmful.

Let's take a closer look at the words of Step Four: "Made a searching and fearless moral inventory of ourselves" The word "moral" implies that we are embarking on a spiritual search, not a physical one. I often look into the mirror to check my physical self. How is my hair, clothes, weight, posture, face, and the like? However, most of us don't look into the mirror of our souls to see how we stand as someone who can choose good over bad, right over wrong.

The word "inventory" implies a non-judgmental, objective list. I want to find out—as objectively as I can—exactly what my good traits are and those that require improvement. I need to formulate a clearer vision of myself and my actions in order to focus on the hard work of change. If I have a distorted picture of myself, it will be difficult to function properly, and I may become frustrated and depressed.

You should work this step in your own way and at

your own pace. The goal is to develop an honest and undistorted picture of your actions and of your character. What are you like now? What are your strengths? What are your weaknesses? What are you doing that is healthy? What is harmful? It is a good idea to write down your inventory. Begin by making mental notes, and then actually write out your list. It's an amazingly helpful way of looking at yourself.

I have discovered that I am a very caring person but have strong codependent urges. As I have mentioned previously, often my impulse is to try to mold people to be the way I want them to be. I expected my daughter to do her homework in advance of the due dates for reports and projects. My pushing and her delaying always led to arguments. Then, once when she had a report due, I held back from nagging. It was very hard for me to keep quiet as she worked late at night and set her clock for 5:00 AM to complete the report that I would have done at least a few days earlier. Her style is not my style, but she did get the work done and we did not have to fight about it. I even admired her for her fortitude in working to complete the report.

My codependent tendencies also caused me to get angry quickly. From my inventory I could see that my anger is also easily sparked when I feel my pride is hurt. When I examine my inventory, I ask myself: What type of person do I really want to be? What type of person does the Torah tell me to be? I try to be honest in my evaluations, and I have discovered both strengths and weaknesses in myself. I decided that while I want to be a caring, nurturing person, I also want to be more accepting of others. And I definitely want to have more control of my anger.

I now understand that the only person I can change is me. I try not to blame myself or strive for perfection. I intend to grow as a thinking human being who makes better and healthier choices. Looking at how I have been in the past and comparing it to how I would like to be helps me make the right decisions.

Choosing to Be Conscious

Step Four is about reflection. There are many things that stop us from changing. Inertia tends to keep us going in the same direction. In addition, our physical drives and desires are very powerful. If we do not take time to reflect and make moral choices, we can easily fall into the habit of following our physical desires for food, sex, power, and comfort. If we do not make a periodic inventory of ourselves, our ability to make moral choices, which is the essence of being human, could be lost.

Before I started to work on Step Four, I did not even know that anger was something that I could hope to control. And, I automatically tried to change and mold everyone in my family never imagining I had a choice. Now I know that I cannot just follow my natural impulses.

Human beings are not as simple as animals. We have two aspects to our nature. One aspect is our physical/material side. The other is our spiritual/ knowing side. Because I would like to be an aware, fully conscious thinking being, I choose not to just follow my physical urges.

Many of our strongest drives and desires are phys- ical. These desires are often so powerful that we can become enslaved to them as we try to satisfy them. Then our minds will serve our bodies, and we will crush our spiritual natures. As Rabbi Yonah states in the *Gates of Repentance* (1:30): "As long as one follows desire, one is influenced by material consideration and is drawn away from the path of reason."

By making choices based on reason and sound principles, you can master your desires. Rabbi Yonah explains how we can focus or order our physical de- sires so that they are channeled in the right direction.

Rabbi Yonah comments that desire implanted in a person's heart is the root of all one's actions. Therefore, if one's desire is in proper order, instead of being served by all of the body's parts, it will cause them to follow the dictates of intelligence, with which they will become allied and which they will serve. Then all of one's actions will be upright, as it is said, "But as for the pure, his actions are straight (upright)" (*The Gates of Repentance*, 1:31).

We feel desire all the time. We often lack something and want to fill in what is missing. We feel very compelled to fulfill our physical and emotional desires. We eat when we are hungry, sleep when we are tired, yell and make demands when someone disturbs our comfort.

If our lives revolve around fulfilling our bodily needs and comforts, we might not even notice the requirements of our souls, which are not physical but spiritual and intellectual.

We can nourish our souls by learning about the ways of G–d and His world and by acting according to this knowledge and according to His will. We can deliberate and make choices based upon what we know is right, even if it is a more difficult or uncomfortable choice. We can choose to work on changing and improving ourselves, even if it may be frustrating and painful.

I decided to bring my ninety–one year old grandmother to come live with us in our house. I knew that this would make life more difficult for everyone in the house. Someone needs to be home at almost all times, including Shabbat and holidays. It is difficult to plan an outing or family vacation. As a codependent, I knew that it would be a challenge to balance being a caregiver to yet another person while not becoming controlling, and still finding time to take care of myself. However, the alternative for her would have been a nursing facility and I knew this was her greatest fear. I made the choice, even though the result was sure to be more difficult and uncomfortable for me, because I felt that we could do it successfully, and I knew it was right.

These choices are uniquely human, and through them we grow and satisfy the requirement of our souls. We could rush through our lives on automatic pilot, with hardly a thought about who we are as conscious, thinking human beings. As Rambam says, " Awake, awake, oh sleepers, from your sleep" (*Mishne Torah*, Sefer Hamada, Hilchot Teshuva 3:4). If we don't live consciously it is as if we are all asleep. When we have a problem, very few people look inward and reevaluate themselves. The tendency is to regard the problem as happenstance and then to try to distract ourselves from our discomfort. Maybe someone close to us disappointed us or we lost someone we loved. Perhaps we could not get the job we hoped for or we find ourselves in the midst of a financial disaster. We listen to music, go to the movies, eat or take a drink —anything but concentrate on our problem. When we experience a break from our routine, maybe we will think, reflect, and do some *teshuva*.

Yom Kippur, the Day of Atonement, is an entire day set aside for confession and turning to G-d. It follows Rosh Hashanah, when we reinforce our connection to G-d's will. Step Four tells us: Break your routine. Don't wait until the *shofar* sounds to reflect and do *teshuva*. Creating a moral inventory is part of doing *teshuva*. Taking a closer look at yourself is essential to being able to change yourself and become closer to G–d with the ability to make correct moral choices as He intended.

This is the essence of the Fourth Step. You can take this Step anytime you feel ready and confident about yourself and your connection to G–d's wisdom. Working on the first three Steps will give you the confidence to take this Step.

The Torah As Our Guide

What will you put on your inventory? What character traits and actions are important? On what will you focus your attention and energy? How will you evaluate the list you have made?

It is difficult to know what to look for in a personal inventory. Put everything that seems important to you on your inventory. At the same time, remember that the goal is to learn to act out of conscious, deliberate choice instead of reacting out of habit. Examine your habits to see if they are deliberately formed and healthy or automatic and unhealthy. Do you automatically scream when you are irritated, or can you control your expression of anger? I know that one of my problems is getting angry and lashing out. I have now developed the habit of closing my eyes and waiting (some people count to ten), so that I can calm down enough to choose how to express my anger.

Sometimes I simply remove myself from the pres-

ence of other people and think about how to say
something in a way that would be received better.
Making an inventory is a way to look at and sort out
which characteristics and actions are the result of
deliberate choice.

How can we learn to act by deliberate choice? How
can we formulate a plan with a sense of true direction,
instead of stumbling around in the darkness? What
can we do to increase our odds of finding the right
path? Is there a way to determine what is good and
what is bad for our lives?

A good place to begin examining our lives is by
looking in the Torah, the best available instruction
manual since it was given to us by the One who created life itself. The Torah points us in G-d's direction.
Its guidelines clarify characteristics which are worth
attaining.

In the Torah portion of Ki Tissa, (Exodus 34:5-6),
G-d's Thirteen Attributes are provided so that we can
use them as our personal model. The attributes are: be
compassionate, gracious, slow to anger, abundant in
kindness and truth, preserver of kindness, forgiver of
wrongdoings, willful sin and errors and cleaner of the
wrongs of those who do *teshuva*. Jewish tradition tells
us that we all have the potential to become holy and
more similar to G-d, in our character traits.

The chapters of *Pirke Avot* add many positive and
negative character traits to the list. Among these are:
to be a person searching for truth (1:18); someone who

judges others and themselves favorably (1:6); someone who strives for acceptance (6:6), humility (4:4), honesty, and gratitude (3:1); someone who is not hungry for honor, power or revenge (6:5); and one who maintains his or her distance from pride, anger, greed, lust, gluttony, envy, and laziness (2:15, 4:1,28).

I study books such as *Pirke Avot*, Rabbi Yonah's *Shaare Teshuva* (*The Gates of Repentance*), Rambam's *Sefer Hamadah* (*The Book of Knowledge*), Moshe Chaim Luzzato's *Mesillat Yesharim* (*The Path of the Just*) and Eliyahu Dessler's *Michtav Me-Eliyahu* (*Strive for Truth*). These books are guides for good *midot* (traits) and the ways to attain them. Bad or defective character traits will enslave us to serve our physical desires. Good or healthy traits will free us to nourish our souls and serve G–d.

Rambam cautions us to stay clear of extremes in temperament. The best course, he says, is one of balance and moderation.

"...to cultivate either extreme in any class of dispositions is not the right course, nor is it proper for any person to follow or learn it...The right way is the middle path in each group of dispositions common to humanity...Our ancient sages exhorted us that a person should always evaluate his dispositions and adjust them to be at the mean between the extremes, and this will insure his physical health. Therefore, a person should not be easily moved to anger, nor be like the dead without feeling, but should aim at the happy medium. Be angry only for a grave cause that rightly calls for anger, so that what was done will not be done again" (*Mishne Torah*, Sefer Hamadah, Hilchot Deot 1:3–4).

In his classic book, *The Path of the Just*, Rabbi Moshe Chaim Luzzato tells us that, according to the Talmud, we should develop the trait of watchfulness (*zehirot*). We must contemplate and evaluate all of our behavior and be careful in our actions.

The idea of watchfulness, Luzzato says, is for one to exercise caution in one's actions and one's under–taking. To be deliberate and watch over one's actions and one's accustomed ways to determine whether or not they are good, so as not to abandon one's soul to the danger of destruction, and not to walk according to habit, as a blind man in pitch darkness....

Luzzato tells about Jeremiah who complained about the evil of the men of his generation, about their being blinded to their actions, and their failure to analyze them in order to decide whether they should be continued or abandoned. Jeremiah says about these men: "No one regrets his wrongdoing...They all turn away as a horse rushing headlong into battle" (Jeremiah 8:6). Luzzato alludes to running on the impetus of their habits without leaving themselves time to evaluate their actions, and, as a result, falling into evil without even noticing it (*Mesillat Yesharim*, chapter 2).

This teaches us that we must not simply act on

impulse or out of habit. It is essential to make a searching and fearless moral inventory of ourselves. Then we
will be able to refer to Torah guidelines for a clearer
picture of what it means to be a human being guided
by reason and deliberate action. This will enable us to
formulate a plan for better and healthier actions.

My Inventory

When I began to contemplate my actions, I discovered that one of my defects is my difficulty in
trusting my judgment when others disagree, even
when the truth is obvious. This is a stumbling block
against faith in G-d and His system. Trust in the truth
needs to be stronger than any trust in people or in
their opinions.

When my daughter was four, I decided that what
she needed was to go to a nursery school on a part-
time basis. I went to a school and told them I was
looking for a program that was half-day, three days a
week. They offered only five-day programs. I told them
that my daughter was not ready for a five-day program. They replied that perhaps her mother was not
yet ready for this program. I was confident in my judgment of my daughter's needs and went elsewhere.
Three days of nursery school worked out very well for
her. When it was time for kindergarten, she was ready
and happily went to a full five day program.

I was confident in my ability to know what was
right for my daughter. However, I was not yet confi-

dent in my ability to know what was right for me. I
was filled with doubt as to whether this Torah lifestyle
I had chosen was actually correct. So many people had
questioned my judgment. I had to search fearlessly to
come to realize that I also know what is right for me,
regardless of what other people may say. The ability to
make good choices for myself comes from making
decisions that are based on Torah and reason.

Dr. Blema Feinstein convinced me to join her at a
Shabbaton (Sabbath weekend retreat) to hear Rebbetzin Tzippora Heller speak. Rebbetzin Heller is an
excellent and insightful lecturer who teaches at Neve
Yerushalayim, a women's yeshiva in Israel. While we
waited for one of her lectures, I told Dr. Feinstein of the
difficulty I had in believing in the truth of G–d and
Torah. I had been struggling with what I thought was
a problem of faith. Although I kept trying to find proof
of G–d's existence and the truth of Torah, I never felt
satisfied. After some discussion, I explained how difficult it was for me to follow a belief and a way of life
that so few people were following. I felt that I was
joining the smallest minority in the world, in the
U.S.A., within the Jewish people, and even within my
family. My problem suddenly became clear—I did not
have enough faith in my own ability to evaluate information and make good choices for myself.

Within minutes of this discussion, Rebbetzin
Heller began to speak. She told us that we often look
at ourselves in a mirror and are satisfied with the way

we look. Then if someone comments on how good we look, we feel terrific. If someone comments on how bad we look, we feel terrible. We know how we look. The problem is that we do not always trust our own judgment. She continued to talk about how we face the same problem in spiritual matters. It was exactly what I needed to hear.

The heaviness of my doubts began to lighten. I realized that I could trust my judgments and choices, because I was making careful and deliberate decisions based on the truth of Torah. I was not acting on impulse or out of habit. I did not have to accept the judgments and influences of the outside world. I could take time to make a moral inventory. I could be a person who makes deliberate and reasonable decisions.

I try to take some time out in the week to formulate general goals on which to focus my daily actions and a plan of implementation by asking myself questions. What is G–d's will for me? What do I need to do to gain more control of my life, be happier and live a more spiritually satisfying life? I try to keep the resulting ideas in mind as I go through each day, to keep more of my actions deliberate and goal oriented. I am not on such a high level that I deliberate with everything that I do. Just being more aware helps me make more conscious choices.

Making Choices

I found confidence in my ability to make choices.

With Torah models and commandments as my guide, I found I could be true to my spiritual nature.

When we honestly work to remove the distortions about how we thought life was supposed to be (based on society's values and misconceptions), we begin to understand the way things really are. We can see more clearly who we have harmed and how we have been harmed. We can see who we have helped and how we have been helped. Becoming the master of our thoughts and actions allows us to become precious and free to live life as G-d intended—as moral human beings created in His image with the ability to think and freely choose what is good and right.

When we live with a clear sense of reality, we can appreciate ourselves for who we are. When we act more in accordance with the way G-d intended human beings to act, we become more precious to ourselves, to others, and hopefully to G-d.

Begin taking your moral inventory, and you will be able to accomplish more than you may have thought possible.

Step Five

**Admitted to G-d,
to ourselves, and to
another human being
the exact nature
of our wrongs.**

✦ ✦ ✦

Looking Outward

In Step Four, we examined the concept of a moral inventory. By discovering our spiritual selves we can better decide what is needed to make the right choices for our lives. In Step Five, we delve into this further.

Step Five

Admitted to G-d, to ourselves, and to another human being the exact nature of our wrongs.

This step is a three-pronged process; first we must look deeply at ourselves, then we must acknowledge trust in the inherent goodness of G-d, and finally we must be willing to ask for and accept help from others.

In the daily prayers, in the silent devotion of *Shemoneh Esrei*, we say, "Forgive us Father, for we have erred. Pardon us, our King for we have willfully sinned."

Thus you can see that Jews who pray daily acknowledge in their prayers the error of their ways to G–d.

Step Five focuses on confession, honesty, humility, and forgiveness. When we have done something harmful, this can weigh heavily upon us. In order for confession to lift this weight, it must be absolutely honest and truthful. In speaking the truth, we become more aware of our deficiencies, and this often results in a sense of humility. We may then also become more aware of the need to forgive people who have harmed us and to ask forgiveness of those we have harmed. Often forgotten at this point is the need to also forgive ourselves for harm we may have brought upon ourselves or for not being as perfect as we'd like to be.

Jews who pray regularly, may have already done some work on this Step, since, as I mentioned, confession to G–d is a part of daily prayers. In addition, turning to G–d is a regular focus of those who make prayer part of their lives. It is the direction of the *teshuva* process. In order to change, we first need to admit that we are on the wrong path.

Some people wait a long time before they consider changing their ways and confessing their wrongdoings. Many wait for the confessions of Yom Kippur. On days such as Yom Kippur and other yearly fast days, complete *teshuva* is especially encouraged. These days help us contemplate our ways. However, any day we pray, is a good day to confess our sins.

Working Step Four entails making mental and written lists about our character traits and our actions. Step Five asks us to utter the words of our wrongdoings aloud. Saying the words is important, because it helps clarify our problems. It also brings the wrongdoing outside ourselves so we can work on it and thus rid ourselves of it.

Help From a Friend

Finding a trusted advisor is an essential part of the Twelve Step program. We start by talking to another person since lack of practice and lack of humility often make it difficult to know what we should confess and how we must confess. Even for people experienced in establishing a relationship with G–d through daily prayer, it is still important to find a trustworthy person to confide in. The right person can keep us honest and point out things about us we may not realize.

Who is the right person? Where can you find an advisor? How often do you need to consult with an advisor?

Every person will have a different answer for these questions. Only you will know what is right for you. Some people find a sponsor or advisor in their Twelve Step meetings, where members who have been in the program for a while will offer to be the sponsor or advisor for someone else. Some people form trusted friendships in the meetings and advise and support each other. In some families, there is an older or wiser member who comes to be an advisor for other members of the family. Traditionally, people have also turned to rabbis and teachers as advisors.

How often you consult an advisor is also a individual choice, usually determined by one's need and one's available time. You may talk to someone every day if you are in a crisis and your advisor has the time and inclination. When life is easier, or perhaps just busier, you might go many months without needing your advisor's help.

For me, Dr. Blema Feinstein has been both a trusted friend and an advisor. She helps me see things about myself that are often hidden from my view. Once I went to speak with her when I was unhappy about my marriage. She helped me to see that I suffered from many illusions about the very institution of marriage. I was still living under the "Cinderella illusion," that when two people marry, they live happily ever after without cares and troubles. I also had mistakenly believed that a married couple must enjoy all of the same activities and do everything together. (I don't even know where this one came from!)

Dr. Feinstein helped me understand that these expectations were unrealistic and then she helped me mourn the loss of my misconceptions so that I could finally let them go. A clear view of reality gave me a totally different picture. I am a very independent person and enjoy being alone. In fact, if I am with people for a long time, I crave solitude. If I had the marriage of my illusion, I would probably be stifled and miserable.

Once I broke through this illusion, I could see the many benefits in my marriage. In fact, I discovered that my husband is exactly the husband that I need. (G–d, in His infinite wisdom created us in such a way that most of us get married when we are young and foolish. Otherwise, we might choose the spouse that our illusions and misconceptions tell us we want!)

Ideas are very powerful. False ideas made me unhappy. I had so many misconceptions about my future. I was supposed to get married, have lots of children, enjoy all of the things my husband enjoys, never have troubles, have a wonderful job, lots of money and, of course, live happily ever after. Now every time I begin to think of something that I am supposed to do or have, I look critically to see if this is yet another illusion creeping into my life. Talking to a good advisor enabled me to break through my many illusions, so that I could begin to see reality clearly.

Confessing to Others and to G-d

According to Jewish tradition, there are definite times when one should confess to another person one's wrongdoings. It is based on the idea stated in the twenty–eighth proverb: "If one person has sinned against another, he must confess and ask for forgiveness. If one person sins against G–d in a public way, so that people know about it, he is required to confess in front of others in order to sanctify G–d's Name."

Rabbi Yonah reminds us: The Sages of Israel have interpreted "He who hides his offenses shall not prosper" as applying to sins such as those between one person and another, which are not forgiven until the sinner has returned items he has stolen, seized, or robbed, or has asked forgiveness of anyone he has oppressed or shamed or slandered. The verse is applied also to transgressions between man and G–d which have become known to others.

Rabbi Yonah points out: "One who transgresses openly, desecrating the Name of G–d, must regret and mourn over his transgression in the presence of others so that His Name is sanctified" (*The Gates of Repentance*, 1:8).

In addition, Psalm 50 stresses the importance of confession in rectifying our relationship to G–d. Even at the time of the *Bait HaMikdash* (Holy Temple) in Jerusalem, a sacrifice was useless if it was offered to G–d without thought or heart.

King David tells us that before we can make our sacrifice we must first confess to G–d. "Confess to G–d and then pay your vows to the Most High" (Psalms 50:14).

Through confession, we honor G–d and we will benefit from His help. "He who confesses honors Me and I will put him on the path and show him G–d's deliverance" (Psalms 50:23).

Rambam repeatedly underscores the importance

of confession. In Numbers (5:6-7) we are told: "When a man or woman commits any sin that men commit against the Lord, and that person is guilty, then they shall confess their sin which they have done." This, Rambam emphasizes, means to confess in words... "The fuller and more detailed the confession one makes, the more he is praiseworthy... Even if people have made restitution, received punishment, or brought a sacrifice they are not forgiven...until they have repented and made confession in words" (*Mishne Torah*, Sefer Hamadah, Hilchot Teshuva 1:1).

Praying gives us the opportunity and the language to confess our wrong doings to G–d. I had a very hard time composing the words that I needed. I turned to my prayer book and found a paragraph that could be inserted into the *Shema Koleinu* prayer. I began to insert this prayer every time I recited the *Shemoneh Esrei*, making a confession of my anger. I asked G–d to forgive all the things I had done wrong since I was a child and to repair anything I had damaged.

Change did not come immediately for me. However, gradually I have felt my anger being removed from within. I do not hide my anger or hold it inside any longer. This is not only harmful to me but also to others. I can assert my desires and accomplish what I need to accomplish while remaining calm. Anger is no longer my automatic response to minor irritations.

Confession can ease a troubled past and a sense of

isolation. When we talk and listen to people in confidence, it is comforting to hear how many others share our difficulties. Trustworthy advisors keep us in check and let us know that there is someone available to help us. Talking to G–d reminds us that He is always there to sustain us.

The Exact Nature of My Wrongs

The second part of this step is ascertaining the exact nature of your wrongs. *Exact* indicates something very precise. This step does not say exact details, but exact "nature." This does not mean that you should only make a list of all the wrong things you have done, but that you must also search for the *nature* of your wrong doings. What is the precise underlying flaw or lack of understanding that leads you to act badly? You know that you have done something wrong because of the outcome of your actions: you did not accomplish what you had intended, or someone was hurt by what you did. I have discovered that I often know that I have done something wrong without understanding the real problem or the exact *nature* of my wrong.

Judaism and the Twelve Steps teach us that when our physical desires control us, they prevent us from developing healthy traits (see Step Four). The Twelve Step program considers physical addictions such as alcohol, drugs, and gambling to be our physical desires. Also included would be emotional addictions such as those exhibited by codependents and ragea-holics. Rabbi Moshe Chaim Luzzato often discusses the negative character traits of pride, anger, envy, and lust. Rambam stated that such negative traits expressed a sickness of the soul.

We could add to this list the strong desires for comfort, honor, and wealth. These characteristics and desires block us from developing healthier behaviors such as patience, kindness, and honesty which would bring us closer to G-d. It becomes impossible to develop our understanding and connection to G-d while we are in the grip of physical desires. When we act against G-d's will, we are hurting ourselves, others and our connection to Him.

My problem of trying to control everything became apparent because I was often anxious and unable to take care of myself physically. I had both stomach and back problems that I was trying to ignore, even though they kept getting worse. Slowly, I came to the realization that my controlling behavior was the symptom. The exact nature of my wrong, the sickness of my soul, was that I did not have enough understanding of G-d to realize that it is in G-d's power to control the universe. I was attempting to do it myself. I also did not understand G-d's goodness. Since everything G-d creates is good, this included the people I was trying so desperately to take care of. In fact, it took me a while to learn that they are so good that they could take care of themselves.

What I still lacked was a deep understanding that went beyond intellectual knowledge. Experience and acceptance of G–d's power and goodness was necessary. There had to be a way for me to become aware of G–d's presence in the world, so that I could trust in His control.

First I listened to others in my CODA meeting talk about their own lives. Then, I slowly began to let go of controlling others. I soon observed how the world could function without my total involvement.

It took me a long time to understand what a small part of the universe I am, and this lack of understanding added to my inability to control my anger. My desire for physical comfort, honor, and power often led to misdirected anger. Grave offenses which would have perhaps justified my anger did not happen that often. Someone embarrassing me, for example, threatened my sense of honor. My daughter or even a student questioning my authority compromised both my desire for honor as well as my desire for power. In the past, I automatically reacted in anger. When I was tired or busy, my anger also used to ignite quicker.

When we do the wrong thing, we are acting according to our own will. When we follow our desires regardless of G–d's will, we are leaving Him out of the picture. Whether we do something small, such as disappointing someone by missing an appointment, or something big, like murdering someone, we are turning from G–d's will and damaging our connection to

His wisdom. When we talk about fear of G–d (*yirat Hashem*), our greatest danger to ourselves occurs when we damage our relationship with G–d since that is our purpose for being alive. Part of the idea of fear of G–d, is fear of losing our connection to G–d.

We find this idea mentioned many times in the Tanach. In fact, even King David expressed this concern of damaging his connection to G–d. When he sinned, he confessed of his wrongdoing in relation to G–d. In the book of Samuel II, chapters 11 and 12, we are told the story of King David's sin with Bat Sheba. King David wanted to marry Bat Sheba, so he sent her husband off to war. Although everything was arranged legally, in essence, he caused a man's death. The prophet, Nathan, reminds David who he was and the many gifts he had been given by G–d. Nathan asks David, "Why have you despised the word of the Lord, to do that which is evil in His sight?" (Samuel II, 12:9). David had asked to be tested by G–d and failed, but, most importantly, a King of Israel had harmed his relationship with G–d. He confessed to G–d:

"Against You alone have I sinned and I have done that which is evil in Your eyes" (Psalms 51:6).

Step Five then reminds us, as do many examples in the Torah, that we must admit the exact nature of our wrongs to G–d, ourselves, and to another human being. The flaws in our knowledge of G–d and the bad character traits we have developed, which Maimonides calls "sickness of our souls," often lead us in the wrong direction. We need to investigate and uncover the underlying reasons for our wrongdoings. Then we must confess them to G–d, admit them to ourselves, and tell them to a trusted listener or advisor.

There are others out there whom we can turn to for help. It is not necessary to be alone. We can clean the slate and try again. By confessing and strengthening our knowledge of G–d's wisdom, we move closer to G–d. The goal is getting closer, not arriving. The spiritual journey towards G–d and His wisdom leads us away from an empty existence and towards a more fulfilling life.

Step Six

Were entirely ready to have G-d remove all these defects of character.

✦ ✦ ✦

Being Ready for G-d's Help

In Step Five, we entrust the knowledge of our wrongdoings and their exact natures to ourselves, to G-d, and to another human being. We forgive ourselves for not being perfect, recognizing that everything G-d does is for our good, and we turn to and accept the support and assistance of others on our journey toward a better life.

In Step Six, we are ready to accept G-d's assistance in changing ourselves.

Step Six

Were entirely ready to have G-d remove all these defects of character.

Once we do our small part. G-d helps us with the rest. We can pray for G-d's help. And as it is stated in the Talmud (Shabbat 104a):

"Whoever strives for purity is Divinely assisted."

The Midrash Rabbah also notes: "Open for Me an entrance as tiny as a needlepoint and I, in turn, shall open for you an entrance as wide as the entrance of a hall" (Shir Hashirim Rabbah 5:3).

"Let there not be found in us, or in our children, or in our children's children, any defect or disqualification" (*Kel Maleh Rachamim* prayer, *Tashlich* Service).

Being Entirely Ready

Being entirely ready means that we are without doubts and without hesitations. The difficulty in being entirely ready to get rid of our defects is that often we become attached to them. Our style of acting, *even if negative*, has served us to some capacity. Anger, for example, can give us a sense of power or control that we needed at a certain point in our lives. Our perfectionism may have helped us organize an otherwise chaotic situation. The problem is that characteristics we believed were necessary and useful can be harmful to us and get in the way of living a healthy life.

If you feel that your anger serves an important purpose, then you are not entirely ready to give up being angry. If you feel that your family really needs you to take care of them all of the time, then you are not ready to give up control.

You must be entirely ready for G-d's help. This necessitates going through the earlier five steps and coming to recognize that G-d is the only power that can remove our defects. You must begin to recognize that you do not have that power.

If you still feel that all you must do is try a little harder and you'll have more control over whatever your bad habits are, then you are not ready for G-d's help. If you still feel that you only have to be more careful and you won't continue to try to control everyone or be angry or be full of pride (etc.), then you are not ready. If you still believe that you have the power to change yourself by yourself, you are not ready for Step Six.

It is important to rely on G-d as the only real Power and clearly understand your strengths and limitations as human beings before you can begin to feel better about yourselves, without needing to indulge in physical urges or addictions. You can raise your self-esteem. If you feel good about yourselves, you will not feel threatened. The defects are no longer needed to protect a poor self image or to help you survive the battles of life.

Rabbi Abraham Twerski explains in his book, *Let Us Make Man*, that the Israelites complained and rebelled so vehemently in the desert because they suffered from low self-esteem. They did not question G-d's abilities to bring them to *Eretz Yisroel*; rather they doubted that they deserved G-d's help. In other words, they were still thinking like slaves. It took the experience of living in the desert for forty years to remove the defects of these former slaves.

Our forefather Jacob also struggled with self-

doubt, wondering if he was entitled to G–d's assistance. He returned to Canaan with his wives and children and worried about his forthcoming encounter
with his brother Esau, who had sworn to kill him. The
Torah tells us, "And Jacob was very much afraid and
was distressed" (Genesis 32:8). Jacob feared that he
may have used up all his merit and would no longer
merit G–d's help. He addressed G–d and said, "I have
become too small from all the kindnesses and all the
faithfulness which You have already rendered to Your
servant..." (Genesis 32:11). Only after his struggle with
the angel did Jacob come to realize that he still could
and, in fact, should rely upon G–d.

I know it wasn't easy for me to be entirely ready
to give up my tendency to be in charge all of the time,
especially when it came to my household and family.
I couldn't bear the thought that my family would not
eat when I was at work. Knowing that no one could
cook, do the dishes or the laundry as well as I could
actually made me feel good *in spite of* my exhaustion
and frustration. So, I would rush home during my dinner hour to prepare dinner for my family and then try
to clean up and get back to work on time. Of course,
this was not the relaxing hour that I needed and by
the time I got home at 10:00 p.m., I was exhausted.
Even though I could clearly see that this schedule was
not good for me, my family, or my job, I had to
become more ready to let go and leave my family on
their own. I had to trust my family and rely on G–d to

help me out of my codependency.

This is a lesson for all of us. Our lives would be a lot less stressful if we would rely upon G-d more. Each of us can become ready for his or her defects to be removed. And it's best not to pick one or two. All defects are related to enslavement to physical drives, as we discovered when we worked on Step Four.

According to Rabbi Yona and Rabbi Luzzato, it is our physical drives and our preoccupation with material consideration that draws us away from reason and spiritual concerns.

"The earthiness and materialism of this world is the darkness of night to the mind's eye and causes a man to err in two ways" (Luzzato, *Mesillat Yesharim*, chapter 3).

"For as long as a man follows desire, he is influenced by material consideration and is drawn away from the path of reason" (Rabbi Yona of Gerona, *The Gates of Repentance*, 1:30).

These drives block our ability to increase our knowledge about G-d and His ways in the world. By turning to G-d as the source of help, we are focusing on spiritual matters and have already begun to work on the nature of our problems.

There are many characteristics we can work on, many defects of character that perhaps after much soul searching you'll find you have. Changing these things is difficult. Being angry, for example, was a habit that often served no purpose for me. Anger did

not help me accomplish anything. It harmed me physically by making me both tired and frustrated after
each angry outburst, as well as irritating my already
painful stomach condition. It was harmful to my relationships with those I love. Rambam, in the *Mishne
Torah*, warns us to distance ourselves from both pride
(arrogance or haughtiness) and anger.

There are some dispositions to which it is forbidden merely to keep to the middle path. They must be
shunned to the extreme. One such disposition is
pride.... Our sages exhorted us, "Be exceedingly, exceedingly lowly of spirit" (*Pirke Avot* 4:4). The Sages
also stated that anyone who permits his heart to swell
with pride has denied the essential principle of our
religion, as it is said, "and your heart will be proud,
and you will forget the Lord, your G-d" (Deuteronomy, 8:14).

Anger, too, is a negative passion, and should be
avoided. One should train oneself not to be angry
even for something that may justify anger. The
ancient sages said, "He who is angry—it is the same
as if he worshiped idols." They also said, "One who
yields to anger, if he is a sage, his wisdom departs
from him" (*Mishne Torah*, Hilchot Deot 2:3).

Arrogance, pride and anger are deceptive emotions. What sometimes appears as pride or anger may
not be those emotions at all. People who dress well
and deport themselves with an air of confidence may,
in fact, have a great deal of humility. A stern facade

may be an attempt to guide a child without necessarily being an expression of an angry interior. An appearance of extreme humility could be a manifestation of hidden pride. A calm exterior could be masking raging inner turmoil.

You may have to search your heart to determine what is really going on inside. Rabbi Moshe Chaim Luzzato clarifies the types and degrees of what he calls "pride, anger, envy and lust—all evil traits" (*Mesillat Yesharim*, chapter 11). It is beyond the scope of this book to go into great detail in this area, but I will try to summarize some of the main distinctions of these very destructive emotions.

Concerning pride, we are told in the Torah, "and your heart will be proud and you will forget the Lord, your G-d" (Deuteronomy 8:14). Rabbi Luzzato defines pride as follows: "pride consists of a person's pluming himself with his self and considering himself worthy of praise" (*Mesillat Yesharim*, chapter 11).

According to Rabbi Luzzato, we are in danger whenever we take credit for anything good that happens in the world. There are different manifestations of pride, and they all have the potential for causing us to think that we are so great that we can forget about G-d as the ultimate source of goodness. As you can see, this is quite different from getting pleasure from a job well done. Look at the following list. All of these examples are based on the descriptions given by Rabbi Luzzato.

Examples of Pride

Here are some examples of pride:

1) I deserve praise because I am impressively unique (intelligent, handsome, wise, clever, honored). I will conduct myself with great pompousness and be very careful with whom I will associate. Some people may call this arrogant.

2) I deserve praise and I will demean anyone who would dare to bother me with conversation or requests.

3) Since I am so great, I no longer need honor. I will impress everyone with my humble actions.

4) I want to be renowned for all of my fine qualities, including my great humility. I will shun all imposing titles and refuse all dignities, so that all will know that there is no wiser or humbler person in all the land.

5) I may not show it, but in my heart, I know that there are not many who can hope to be as wise as I.

While pride manifests itself in various forms, there are many degrees to anger, ranging from extremely harmful to a level which is so under control that the rabbis would say it was praiseworthy. Although most of us will not be able to reach the final level, according to Rabbi Luzzato, the goal is to be completely clean of anger. According to Maimonides, the only exception is the rare occasion when anger can prevent a recurring infraction of a law or commandment. "Be angry only for a grave cause that rightly calls for anger, so that what was done will not be done again" (*Mishne Torah*, Sefer Hamada, Hilchot Deot 1:4). When Pinchas killed the Israelite Zimri and the the Midianite Cozbi for their immoral and illegal cohabitation (Numbers 25: 6–8), his anger (really zealous for G–d) was completely, absolutely for the sake of heaven. Justified anger like this example, is so rare that many of us will never encounter such a situation in our entire lifetimes.

The following examples are also based on Rabbi Luzzato's descriptions in *Mesillat Yesharim* (ibid). Rabbi Luzzato does not even address the idea of justified anger. Perhaps this is because we are only too ready to feel that all our anger is justified. Remember, real anger, the kind that you feel in your heart, is almost never justified.

Levels of Anger

Here is a listing of levels of anger. Take a look and see if you identify with any of these levels.

1) I am the furious person. I am angered by any opposition to my will. My heart gets so filled with anger that my judgment vanishes. It is this kind of anger that the sages describe as idol worship.

2) I do not get angry over every opposition to my will. Although I am difficult to anger, once I am angry, I am also difficult to appease. Many times I cannot fix what I have damaged in a fit of anger.

3) My anger is not easily incited and even when I am angry, I do not explode. My anger is more restrained. However, I hold and nurse the anger in my heart.

4) It is difficult to make me angry. When I do get angry it is very mild and lasts no longer than a minute. As soon as I realize what is happening, I let it go. My nature moves me to anger, but it no longer lingers inside me, but passes and departs. Although I am not absolutely clean of anger, this is the only way to deal with anger that is healthy and praiseworthy.

5) I am like Hillel, never taking offense and never feeling even a stirring of anger. When I have to reprimand someone, my purpose is only to set them on the right path. Even if my face seems angry, there is no anger in my heart.

After pride and anger, envy, desire and lust are described by Rabbi Luzzato as being self destructive. Envy is completely wasteful, since the one who envies never gets what he wants. Those who envy only harm themselves through their worry, suffering and sinking spirits at seeing someone else's good situation. Closely related are desire and lust. Rabbi Luzzato points out how desires are almost never fulfilled, especially the main desires for wealth and honor. They only cause weariness and draw people away from serving G–d, as they expend all their time and energy on trying to get what they want.

My big character flaw was definitely anger, and I

was stuck at level two. I did not get angry at every opposition to my will, but once I exploded, I nursed my anger for quite some time.

I remember having an argument with my daughter when she was a young child. Within minutes she was calmly playing with her toys. I was still tense and anxious long after the incident. This showed me how harmful anger was to my health and what little effect it had on my daughter's behavior. So I made up my mind to cast off my anger. Easy to say. Difficult to do. I had resolved not to be angry, only to catch myself in the midst of my anger. Perhaps I was trying to jump right to the highest level, to be clean of anger, before I simply learned to control it and let it go. I felt encouraged by the fact that, at least, I had become aware of my anger, instead of simply reacting like a robot.

A desire to change and an increased sense of awareness were not enough to bring about change for me. I had to be ready to make G-d my partner. I had to be ready to ask Him for help. Until I turned to G-d for help, I was only able to recognize my anger with regret. I could not *do* anything to make myself less angry by my will alone.

Whether your problem is anger, like mine, or any of the other negative character traits, remember to be patient. The Twelve Step program is a long process with a lot of work ahead. There are six more steps. This step is only about getting ready. You may not get absolutely clean of all of your negative traits, but you will get a lot healthier if you work the Steps. In later Steps you will start to make the changes that you now recognize as needed.

Defects of Character

Defect implies that something is not as it should be. We are not as we should be. We have some traits that do not suit us. An animal with a blemish was disqualified as a sacrifice in the time of the Bait Ha–Mikdash. Our defects keep us from serving G–d and feeling satisfaction in our lives. Instead, we end up serving our bad habits or addictions.

In the Torah portion of Shoftim (Deuteronomy 28:13), we are warned not to follow the abominations of the other nations. We are told, "Be *tamim* with G–d, your G–d." In the Book of Leviticus, in parshat Vayikra, we are told that the offerings to G–d must be *tamim* and that the individual who presents the offering must also be *tamim*. In the Book of Genesis in parshat Toldot, Jacob is described as an *ish tam*, a man who is *tam*. The Hebrew word *tam* describes a state of wholeness and purity, a being without defects. It also implies a clarity of purpose and a single–minded path, without deviation or distortion. A being that is *tam* is suitable and fulfills its purpose in life.

The animal is a physical being, and its blemish is permanent. It cannot be changed. I am a human being, primarily a thinking being. My purpose is to strive to improve myself, so that I can come to know and serve G-d. My blemishes of character may originate from my physical drives, but unlike animals, these blemishes can be changed. I decided that I was ready to trust in G-d to remove all these defects of character. I knew that I finally was ready to let G-d lead me to being *tam* with G-d, and to live a more satisfied human life.

You, too, must be ready to be free of your defects and to allow G-d to remove them. Being entirely ready is crucial at this point. If you expect help from G-d, you must do your part. Getting ready is the groundwork, the foundation of change. The first six steps involve much introspection, mental work, and preliminary action. In some ways, you may already be changing. The steps are designed to help you get ready to change. You need to realize that you are not in control (Step One), let go and accept G-d as the master (Step Two) and then make His will your will (Step Three). You need to soul search (Step Four) and fix what you have damaged (Step Five). If you do not feel ready, then you need to do more work. Could you honestly expect G-d to help you make changes if you are not ready?

Do you want to change? Do you find you are unable to do so by yourself? Have you acknowledged that you are entirely ready to have G-d remove all these defects of character? The next six steps will involve mental work, but they will also involve more action on your part. If you are ready to change, then you are ready for Step Seven which is to humbly ask G–d for help.

Step Seven

Humbly asked G-d to remove our shortcomings.

✦ ✦ ✦

Asking G-d for Help

Step Six stated that we were entirely ready to let G-d remove all our character faults. And after thinking this through and working on ourselves, we are now prepared to ask Him to do this.

Step Seven

Humbly asked G-d to remove all our shortcomings.

In Step Seven we approach G-d with absolute humility, and acknowledge that only He can remove our defects. On a daily basis, in our prayers, we acknowledge G-d's greatness and our insignificance.

In fact, in the daily morning service we find this exact notion: "Master of all worlds, not in the merit of our righteousness do we pray before you, but in the merit of Your abundant mercy. What are we? What is our life? What is our kindness? What is our righteousness? What is our salvation? What is our strength? What is our power? What can we say before You, G–d, our G–d, and the G–d of our fathers? Are not all the brave nothing before You?...Those who are knowledgeable are as if they had no intelligence? For their many deeds are empty and all of their lives are vanity before you. The superiority of man over beast is nothing because all is vanity. "

Asking Humbly

It took me a long time to find the strength to deal with Step Seven. I had to thoroughly work through the ideas contained in the first six steps, before I could even approach Step Seven. This meant working on my knowledge of G–d and working on my self-knowledge. I had to give up control of my life to Him. I had to hear others talk about asking G–d for His help.

Even though I am continually working on all the earlier steps, I can also approach G–d and humbly ask Him for help in removing my shortcomings. And I have come to understand the many reasons why we should be humble.

First, we have done nothing to earn G–d's help or even merit our creation. Our very existence is possible only because of G–d's never-ending supply of goodness. We exist as human beings through G–d's will and therefore, benefit from His generosity. Whatever goodness we have comes from G–d, because it serves His purpose.

Personally, I also needed to ask G-d humbly to remove my shortcomings. Until now, I have not been the type of person I could have been, the type of person G-d intended me to be. Somewhere along the way, I went astray.

G-d created me with limitless potential. There is so much more for which I can strive. I can have more control over the choices I make. I can act more like someone made in G-d's image. The more good things I discover about myself, the more I realize that compared to G-d, I am nothing.

All my success and all I have obtained have come from G-d. The thought that without G-d's help I am nothing is very humbling. Moshe was our greatest prophet and yet he had great humility. He was so humble that he would "fall on his face" when he approached G-d to ask for forgiveness for the Israelites. He did not have low self-esteem, but simply understood how small he was in comparison to G-d.

In the Torah portion Eikev, in the book of Deuteronomy, the Israelites are reminded that they were given manna in the desert in order to understand firsthand that "it is not by bread alone that man can make a life for himself, but man can live by everything that comes from the mouth of G-d" (8:3).

In his commentary on this portion, Rabbi Samson Raphael Hirsch tells us that it is only an illusion when it seems that our sustenance comes from our physical efforts alone. The manna was supposed to teach us to

put more emphasis on spiritual matters, since we
should acknowledge that whatever possessions we
have come directly from G–d. Hirsch writes, "The
prime factor in man's sustenance is the providence of
G–d. His generous care is evident in every morsel of
bread with which we sustain yet another moment of
our existence. To forget this would mean to fall prey to
a most dangerous delusion upon which our devotion
to duty on earth would flounder. "

The Israelites in the desert are reminded that it
was through no merit of their own that they would
inherit the land of Israel. Only through their ancestors' merits would they be successful in conquering
the land and only because it serves G–d's purpose. The
people who resided in the land of Israel at that time
were wicked and G–d wanted them to be cast out.

The idea that the Israelites inherited the land of
Israel because G–d was keeping His promises to their
ancestors is emphasized in Deuteronomy (9:5–6): "Not
because of your righteousness and because of the
uprightness of your heart are you going there—to take
possession of their land—but because of the wickedness of these nations does G–d—your G–d—drive
them away from before you, and in order to fulfill the
word that G–d swore to your fathers, Abraham, Isaac,
and Jacob. For you must know that it is not because of
your righteousness that G–d—your G–d—is giving you
this good land to take possession, for indeed you are
a stiff-necked people.

Lest there be any doubts, the Torah describes in detail just how rebellious and lacking in merit the Jews were. So, we must humbly ask for G-d's personal intervention because of our ancestors' merit (i.e., Abraham, Isaac, Jacob, Sarah, Rebecca, Leah, and Rachel) and on credit from any future merit of our own. Asking G-d to remove our shortcomings is a valid request because it will enable us to act more in the way that G-d intended us to act. We will train our minds to make deliberate, moral choices, and our bodies will serve our souls. Then we can better serve G-d and His purpose in our world.

Praying for Change

Asking G-d to remove our shortcomings is not a simple request. It is a prayer. It may be a very different type of praying than we are accustomed to doing. Some of us have turned to G-d when we prayed for health. Perhaps we have prayed for a new job or for wealth. Maybe we asked for a spouse or for a healthy child. Often we turn to G-d when we want something.

Now we turn to G-d because we want to *become* something. We'd like to transform ourselves into people who are truly alive as conscious, thinking, choosing human beings. We want to begin the work today and rid ourselves of our shortcomings. Although we can never be perfect, and we will always have shortcomings, we can certainly improve ourselves. Then we can feel precious to G-d and to ourselves, and be free to strive for a healthier and more satisfying life.

Considering my lack of merit, I can only ask. It's impossible to make any demands. There are no guarantees and no time tables. I might see the results of my work and my prayers almost immediately, or it may take many years before some of my shortcomings gradually disappear. I must be patient and trust in G-d.

Each one of our shortcomings will be removed according to G-d's schedule, not any schedule we may have in mind. I am concerned about all of my shortcomings because they are interrelated. I have already greatly improved myself by increasing my understanding of G-d and His world. My defects have already changed to shortcomings. I may be falling short of who I should be, but at least I have a clearer idea of what it means to act the way G-d intended us to act.

I know that my body needs to serve my soul, instead of the other way around. I know I must use my mind to make deliberate moral choices. I have learned that serving G-d's will, doing what is right according to G-d, Torah and true knowledge must take priority over serving my own will. It has taken me some time to understand that I will never accomplish all of this in my physical lifetime, but the goal is to direct my thoughts and actions towards striving to know more of G-d and His ways in the universe.

It also takes time and experience to understand that just being aware of a shortcoming does not guarantee the ability to change. Even if you institute a plan of action, you may find that nothing new happens. Without prayer, without making G-d your partner, change is overwhelmingly difficult, if not impossible.

Before I realized that I could ask G-d for help through praying, I was confused as to why I could not change even if I did not like what I was doing. Whether it was a character trait or habitual behavior, I found myself doing exactly what I did not want to do. This was true even of mundane actions.

For example, when I first became a teacher, I had great ideas about what kind of teacher I wanted to be. To my consternation, when I was finally teaching I found that I was teaching in many of the same ways that I had been taught. My students would talk out of turn. And just like my teachers, I would ask them to write "I will not talk" one hundred times on a piece of paper.

I couldn't figure out how to become the type of teacher that I had intended to be. Patterns were set deeply inside of me. My actions felt automatic, without deliberate thought or choice. Even though I wanted to change, it took enormous effort and fortitude.

Because it was so hard to change what seemed to be simple behavior, I could not imagine controlling major character flaws such as my anger and my need to control everyone. I finally understood that I could not do it alone. I needed help from a power much greater than I.

Using Words

Now I know that I do not have to remove bad character habits and patterns by myself—G–d is my partner. However, I am quite aware that I must work hard and do all that I can and not rely on a miracle. That is why I continue to learn and work on the Twelve Steps. And with total humility I go to G–d and ask Him to remove my shortcomings. Of course, to do this I need to know what to say—I need the right words.

Psalm 51 is particularly well suited for this step. In this Psalm, David asked G–d to remove all his wrongdoings and replace them with a pure heart. "Be gracious to me, G–d, according to Your kindness. According to the abundance of Your mercies blot out my wrongdoings. Wash me thoroughly from my iniquity and from my sin cleanse me…Hide Your face from my sins, and blot out all of my wrongdoings. Create for me a pure heart and renew within me a spirit of correctness" (Psalms 51:3–4, 11–12).

There is a wonderful prayer for *Tashlich* (prayers that are said by the water on Rosh Hashanah) which is recited in a humble tone and covers a variety of shortcomings.

"Please G–d, save us in the merit of Abraham… Isaac…Jacob…Moshe…Aaron…Joseph and David…. May we have composure, quiet, and security so that we may serve You sincerely with no disturbance. Make us worthy of being removed from arrogance, anger, irritability and every kind of conceit. May our minds be at ease....

"May we recognize our insignificance...Let us not be angered or irritated, and may we be lovers of peace and promoters of peace. Make us worthy of being removed from scorn, falsehood, flattery, tale-bearing ...and any form of forbidden speech...Give us strength and health. Make us worthy of being removed from lust and the vain pleasures of this world....

"Make us worthy of being joyful with regard to Your Torah and Your commandments. May our trust be placed in You always and may we have a heart gladdened by Your service...Make us worthy of completing the *tikun* (building, repair) of our lives, spirits and souls" (from *Kel Maleh Rachamim* Prayer, *Tashlich* Service).

I often use my own words. I have asked G-d to remove specific shortcomings. Sometimes I just say, "Please give me the strength and wisdom to do Your will, to walk in Your ways. Please help me to be the way I am supposed to be. I place my shortcomings into Your hands." Whether we use our own words or those of traditional prayers or psalms, it's ideal to actually say our request aloud.

In his book, *The Art of Jewish Prayer*, Rabbi Yitzchak Kirzner stresses the importance of actually verbalizing the words of prayer. Rabbi Kirzner explains that speaking the words removes us from the realm of ideas and brings us closer to the realm of concrete action. The words clarify and crystallize our inner thoughts. When we speak there is more of a sense that we are actually talking to someone and that G–d is actually listening.

Now let's review Step Seven: We need to humbly ask G–d to remove all of our shortcomings. Our humility comes from knowing how small and powerless we are as compared to G–d and from the realization that we can't rely solely on our own abilities. We are concerned with all of our shortcomings because they are all related to our preoccupation with our physical/material existence and cause us to focus on what we think we want instead of what G–d knows we need to become—conscious humans who can make moral choices. We ask with words, because through these words we move from the realm of ideas into the realm of concrete action of approaching and relating to G–d.

By asking G–d for help, our shortcomings will be removed following His schedule. This enables us to live spiritually, with our lives based on reason and a sense of what is right instead of on what we need to merely exist. With such a foundation, our prayers can help us make the changes we need in order to be complete spiritually as well as physically.

Step Eight

*Made a list of all persons
we have harmed, and
became willing to make
amends to them all.*

✦ ✦ ✦

Preparing to Make Amends

Step Four required that we list each of our character traits—good points as well as bad. In Step Seven, we acknowledged G-d as the only Power Who can remove our defects and we realized that we can communicate with Him through formal prayer or in our own words. In Step Eight, we begin to think about making amends for our wrongdoings which in many cases can occur as a result of our character flaws.

Step Eight

Made a list of all persons we had harmed, and became willing to make amends to them all.

Once again, we make a list—this time of all the people we have harmed. But before we even make this list it's important to acknowledge our obligation to make amends. There are many references to looking inward and evaluating ourselves in the Torah: "If I am not for myself, who will be for me? And if I am only for myself, what am I?" (Hillel, *Pirke Avot* 1:14). "You shall not hate your brother in your heart" (Leviticus 19:17).

Making a List

Steps Eight and Nine evolve as a natural result of working on the previous steps. They lead to taking responsibility for all our actions. If we are to make true progress, we must take responsibility for the past. The only way to move forward is to fix all that we have damaged along the way.

We must take a look at the effect of our character traits and the people we may have caused pain or damage because of them.

We can harm others in a great variety of ways ranging from expressing our annoyance to causing permanent emotional or physical damage. We may go into a rage when someone awakens us, or act arrogantly if we make a lot of money.

A child who interrupts our conversation may be reprimanded in a harsh manner. A competitor to our business may be cheated so that we can get ahead. If we are supervising someone, we may denigrate them. We may think, how dare they rob us of our precious time. We may fight with someone over a parking spot or a seat on the bus. If we are codependent, we can control someone so much that they become so dependent they lose their ability to take care of themselves. We can try so hard to make someone better that we crush them with our words or actions.

Step Eight totally benefits us. In order to recover from our previous problems, we must recognize our personal history and the damage that we have done. This way we can attempt to get rid of any buried guilt and shame. This is the time for both absolute honesty and self acceptance.

It is easier to look at something we've done that may have been harmful when we realize that we are *not* the action. You may have actually harmed yourself by acting badly. Thus when we name the people we have harmed, we include our own name. Our first responsibility is to fix ourselves.

I, for instance, know that I have a problem with pride and if I feel in any way dishonored I will burn in anger, leaving me with stomach and head pains resulting from an angry outburst. My desire to control others harms my relationship with others and leaves me feeling isolated and alone. We can only be there for others, if we have taken care of ourselves first. We can only show kindness to others if we have learned not to hurt ourselves.

Getting Ready

The second part of Step Eight is to become willing to make amends to people we have harmed. Before we can move to Step Nine and make amends, we may have to make the changes inside ourselves to become the type of person who is *willing* to make amends to others, including ourselves. This may take a lot of work or it may be an easy process for you— indeed it is harder if you have not worked on all the previous steps.

Different people will find varied prerequisites to being ready to make amends. I discovered that before I could make amends I had three requirements.

1) Being able to control my pride.

2) Having enough humility to forgive others in the heart.

3) Having the ability to love and care for others.

If you, like me, still struggle with the character flaw of undue pride, for instance, then it may be really dif-ficult for you to do this and you may not be ready to make amends to others. Instead of taking responsibil-ity for your actions, you may still be blaming others. You may find yourself with the following thoughts:

+ Why should I make amends?

+ They got what they deserved.

+ It was their own fault.

+ They hurt me, so I was entitled to hurt them back.

+ I am right. In fact, I am not often wrong.

Step Eight is about being willing to make amends to all those you have harmed. We often hurt people as a reaction to what they have done to us. If you cannot forgive them in your heart for their wrongdoings, you are not ready to ask for their forgiveness. If you search your heart and find only anger, you are not ready to make amends. If you feel that you are justified, that it must be someone else's fault, you are not ready to take responsibility for your actions.

Even if you still feel that someone has really wronged you, harboring resentment and not being able to forgive them in your heart will hurt *you*, not them. Remember, they probably also feel justified for their actions.

The only exception is the absolutely evil and idolatrous person. According to Maimonides, there are people who forfeit their rights for our consideration and may even deserve our hatred. There are some very strong commandments against idolaters and those who entice others into idolatry. Maimonides states that there are fifty-one precepts regarding idolatry, including "not to pervert others to idolatry, to burn a town in which the population has been so perverted, not to love the enticer, not to cease hating him, and not to save him from punishment" (*Mishne Torah*, Sefer Hamada, Hilchot Avoda Zarah V'Chukat Hagoyim).

Most of the people we meet will probably not fit into such a hateful category. However, you may have to adjust your character traits to be able to forgive others whom you feel have harmed you. If you need to work on ridding yourself of pride and increasing your humility, keep working on steps four through seven.

If you have enough humility to forgive others, then you are ready to consider whether you have the ability to love others as well as yourself.

"Love your neighbor as yourself" (Leviticus 19:18).

The verse clearly says, I must love my neighbor *as* myself, *not* more than myself. This is not a commandment to sacrifice myself for the sake of others. If I am to love my neighbor as myself, I must first understand what it means to love myself. I must first take care of myself, since only then can I be there for others. Otherwise, I may resent and, perhaps, grow to hate the person for whom I have made such a "sacrifice." To love myself, I have to forgive myself. And in order to love my neighbor, I have to forgive others. This is possible only when I give them the benefit of the doubt and finally acknowledge that no one is perfect.

When I stopped managing my husband's life, I began to see that I could love him even if things were not done my way, even if I felt that his actions were imperfect. Once, while driving our new car, I backed it into the garage door and dented the car. I was afraid my husband would be angry with me because he had told me several times not to back the car into the garage. I wanted him to love me, even though I was not perfect, even though I had messed things up. And yet it took me some time to realize that I was hoping for his unconditional love even though I had not always extended to him this kind of acceptance. (He never did get angry about the dent!)

My husband is a certified public accountant which means that for three months preceding April 15 he is very busy. If he was feeling tired and said some unkind words to me, I would feel insulted and argue with him. After working this step, I was able to see the foolishness of what I was doing. He is entitled to be tired and irritable. He recently said something that made me angry and I responded out of anger. Only this time, I thought about it. I reminded myself about his work situation. Since I was able to forgive him for his remarks, I was able to think about asking his forgiveness for mine. My anger toward him disappeared and was replaced with feelings of love toward him.

I suddenly realized that my need for unconditional love is not unusual—it's a universal desire. It is possible to love others simply because we were all created by G-d, imperfections and all. It is, indeed, possible if we understand and forgive everyone else's imperfections. It is unnecessary to agree with everyone. Each of us has the right to be who we are and to make our own choices and mistakes.

My mother gave me unconditional love and acceptance. Having my mother as a role model strengthened my ability to develop these character traits. When I was angry as a child and told her that I hated her, she would turn to me and say, "Well, I love you." She supported my choices of study as a student. When I became an observant Jew she told me, "I do not understand you, but I respect you and I love you."

There are two parts to Step Eight. Making a list of those whom you have harmed is easy. Finding the ability to love and accept those very people on the list is more difficult but it is essential to being willing to make amends to them all.

Sometimes, making amends to others involves coming to the understanding that no matter what a person's position or title, every human is valuable and deserves to be treated well.

The rabbis in the Talmud (Sanhedrin) say that all of us should realize that the whole world was created for the sake of each individual. This is why saving the life of one person is like saving the whole world. G–d gave us life. Each life is special and precious and enormously valuable. Even if we live out our lives and never discover exactly what G–d intended, we each have a purpose as defined by G–d.

We are responsible to ourselves and to others to respect every individual G–d created. If we consider this idea, we will run from harming anyone or ourselves either physically, emotionally or spiritually. How could you hit or criticize someone you respect or love as one of G–d's creations? How can you steal from someone whom G–d has created? Why would you explode in a rage at a precious individual? Why would you neglect to take care of yourself if you appreciate your own value? If you develop the ability to love and respect others and yourself, you will never consciously harm anyone. Only our habitual reactions cause us to harm others. These are the very habits that can be changed with the help of the Twelve Steps.

Instead of harming others through what may be habitual patterns of behavior, we can attempt to have a life with others based on mutual respect and care. Step Eight is about preparing both a list and ourselves. For some people it could take a long time to get ready to make amends. There may be a lot of inner work that has to be done before we can say, "I'm sorry, please forgive me." We may have to open our hearts and forgive another before we can consider substituting kindness for what may have been previous cruelty.

However, gradually, when we recognize the value of ourselves and others; we will be able to make this list of people we have harmed and be willing to forgive and make amends.

In Step Nine, we will take the necessary action and make those amends. In Step Eight we begin to be more careful about ourselves and others, both mentally and physically so that we may begin to live the way G–d intended when He created us.

Step Nine

Made direct amends to such people wherever possible, except when to do so would injure them or others.

✦ ✦ ✦

Making Amends

In *Step Eight, we prepare ourselves to make* amends for the wrong we may have done to others. We have listed all the people we may have hurt or harmed—including ourselves. Most importantly, we recognize that our first priority is to change ourselves *before* we can begin to make amends to others. Part of the change that enables us to make amends is checking our pride, having enough humility to forgive, and learning to love and value other people enough to make amends for anything we may have done wrong. Once we have done all of this work we are ready for Step Nine.

Step Nine

Made direct amends to such people wherever possible, except when to do so would injure them or others.

In Step Nine we make amends directly to those we have harmed. These are the same people that we had listed in Step Eight. How does one go about making amends? How could amends ever be harmful?

First we will consider why making amends is important for both our recovery and *teshuva* (repentance) and some ways in which making amends is possible. Then we will evaluate if our actions will be helpful to others or if it will inflict further injury. Let us examine some traditional sources which direct us to make amends to those we have wronged.

"Repentance and the Day of Atonement secure forgiveness only for transgressions against G–d...But transgressions against one's fellow–men...are never pardoned until the injured party has received the compensation due him and has also been appeased... Even if a person only annoyed another in words, he has to pacify him and entreat him until he has obtained his forgiveness" (Rambam, *Mishne Torah*, Sefer Hamadah, Hilchot Teshuva 2:9).

Taking Action

There are two parts to doing *teshuva*, or in fact any change:

First we have to work on ourselves on the inside. We can make lists and decisions on how we want to be. We can ask G–d for help and guidance. True change, however, will be incomplete until it affects our *actions*.

The second thing we must do is act. Once we've acknowledged whom we may have hurt, we must go to this person or these people and make amends. In this way, we take responsibility for our past actions and for the well being of others. Often this takes a lot of hard work. We can do this only once we have become strong, caring, and forgiving.

Often when we hurt someone, we feel it was justified because they may have hurt us first. If our wrongdoing is justified, it's difficult to understand the point of asking for forgiveness. Thus first, we have to come to terms with *why* we did the wrong act in the first place. We have to bring ourselves to forgive others for hurting us, and realize that hurting others is *never* justified. It may take a lot of work to forgive those who have hurt us. But only after we forgive them, will we be able to ask them to forgive us.

You may wonder how you can become more caring and forgiving? The best formula is to first build a strong connection to G–d and gain confidence in your own value as a human being. Making amends to people you have wronged makes you stronger by freeing you of accumulated guilt and shame. For years, you may have hurt other people. Somehow you must try to right whatever wrong you have done. Sometimes an apology is all that is needed. You must be kind and concerned where previously you may have been hurtful and given pain. You must try to provide compensation for any losses you caused. These actions can cleanse and purify you.

I recently discovered, for example, that my daughter felt hurt because I was not being a good enough listener. Perhaps I was busy and distracted, but she interpreted the lack of attention as an indication that I did not care about her. I apologized and reassured her that I do care, and now I try to set aside more uninterrupted time for just listening to what she needs to tell me.

The Torah's whole system of justice is based mainly on compensation rather than punishment. Punishment would imply that someone was bad or evil. Compensation implies concern for the person who was harmed. There is a recognition of a wrongdoing that needs to be set right. In the Book of Exodus, in the portion of Mishpatim, laws are given to insure that we live together as a civilized society. Punishment is reserved only for certain crimes.

In crimes of damage and theft, the perpetrator must make amends to the victim. One must compensate the victim for any physical injury by giving the victim the value of what was damaged and the loss incurred. This is what is meant by the expression "an eye for an eye and a tooth for a tooth." We are also told, "eye for eye, tooth for tooth, hand for hand, foot for foot, burn for burn, wound for wound, bruise for bruise" (Exodus 21:24–25).

This notion is repeated throughout the Torah: "If a person opens a pit or if a person digs a pit and does not cover it, and an ox or a donkey falls into it, then the owner of the pit must make restitution, he must restore the full value to its owner..." (Exodus 21:33–34).

"If a person leads one's animals into a field or a vineyard...he shall make restitution with the best of his own field..." (Exodus 22:4). "If a man borrows something from another and it is broken...he must make full restitution" (Exodus 22:13).

These all refer to physical matters. It is more difficult to legislate in matters of the heart and mind, yet the message from the Torah is clear. If you have harmed someone, then you must make amends. Whether it is through an apology or monetary compensation, the focus in this step is on the victim, so be sure to make amends in a tactful way, without inflicting further damage.

What kinds of things do you need to do? Perhaps the following list will help you.

✦ If you harmed someone, you can simply and sincerely say that you are sorry. This means being unambivalently apologetic.

✦ If you have been impatient, apologize and then make an effort to be more patient.

✦ If you were the cause of someone losing a position, a job or money, be prepared to reimburse them or help them find another position.

✦ If you caused someone to think less of another person, go back to them and try to correct that opinion.

✦ If you have been cruel to someone, apologize and then try to treat them in a kinder manner.

✦ If you yelled at someone angrily, apologize and try to speak to them next time calmly, even if you find them irritating.

In Genesis, in the portion of Bereshit, Cain killed his brother Abel. G–d asked him, "Where is Abel, your brother? And he replied: I do not know. Am I my brother's keeper?" (Genesis 4:9). The answer to his question is: Yes, we are our brother's and our sister's keeper. If we want to live as fully conscious, thinking, spiritual, human beings created in G–d's image, then we must take responsibility for our actions and care about others. We must make amends to all those we have harmed.

Step Ten

*Continued to take
personal inventory and
when we were wrong
promptly admitted it.*

✦ ✦ ✦

Continuing a
Personal Inventory

In Step Nine, we directly approach anyone we may have harmed to set things right. Once we've learned how to love and forgive ourselves for our imperfections, it becomes easier to apologize or other–wise compensate anyone who may have been a victim of our wrongdoings.

We have learned to take responsibility to make amends, unless doing so would cause more harm. In Step Ten, we continue to take personal inventory. As we continually observe ourselves, we can quickly see what we do wrong and act quickly to correct our behavior.

Step Ten

Continued to take personal inventory and when we were wrong promptly admitted it.

It's important to always be on guard. It is easy to

fall under the negative influences that bombard us daily. Our society often puts a greater value on wealth and power than on wisdom and kindness. The newspaper may be filled with news about sports, music, television and movie stars and contain little about major world news. Entertainers and sports figures are heralded by the media as our heroes. Without our conscious awareness, these values, or lack of values, may creep into our own belief system. We can never be sure when we have perfected ourselves to a point where we are beyond the influences that cause us to do wrong.

This simply means that we have to be aware of everything we do and make sure it's what we have decided is proper.

Hillel the great thinker reminds us, "Do not be sure of yourself until the day of your death" (*Pirke Avot* 2:5).

Rambam expresses this idea eloquently: "A man should always regard himself as if his death were imminent and imagine that he may die this very hour, while still in a state of sin. He should therefore turn from his sins immediately and not say—I will wait till I am old" (*Mishne Torah*, Sefer Hamadah, Hilchot Teshuva 7:2).

Making an Ongoing Inventory

My life is busy and so my house often becomes cluttered. I can't seem to keep up with the vast number of things that have accumulated. Some things I bought, some I acquired, and some I inherited. Then there are those things whose origin I cannot trace. There are the books, papers, clothes, toys, lamps, furniture, and assorted baby items. Left on its own, the junk seems to grow and have a life of its own. If I don't take inventory from time to time and throw things away, the piles grow higher and more unmanageable. Occasionally, I find something useful or valuable to keep.

The same problem exists with personal traits and actions. The consequences of *not* monitoring ourselves is even more serious. Without an ongoing inventory, our personal lives can become a mess. We can become used to harmful behavior without even realizing it. Negative influences can pile up, and we can easily slip into unacceptable patterns of behavior, such as automatically reacting with anger, arrogance or envy, without conscious thought of what we really know to be right. My main problem is that I'm a codependent and can easily fall into the pattern of criticizing and trying to control other people.

By constantly taking a personal inventory, we can continuously think and choose what we do. We need to be aware of our actions so that when we do something wrong, we can promptly admit it to ourselves and to the person we may have wronged. If we do this, additional conflict and guilt will be avoided.

Getting into the habit of admitting to others we are wrong, helps us act honestly and take responsibility for our behavior. This positive attitude will help us build healthy relationships with others. And admitting our wrongs to G–d helps us build our relationship with Him. Then we can focus on turning toward G–d's will and doing what is right.

Rosh Hashanah and Yom Kippur occur only once a year and are intense times for reflection. For some people, these are the only times during the year they take to reflect and contemplate change. However, taking stock of our lives and being aware of our short-comings can be a daily task. We can spot check ourselves throughout the day. Resolutions can be made each morning. A review can be made at the end of the day. We can periodically take the time to make more thorough inventories. Goals can be revised and there is always more that can be done.

Prayer

Prayer is a part of both Steps Ten and Eleven. However, we can ask G–d for forgiveness at anytime. The formal obligation to pray gives us a scheduled opportunity to connect to G–d, admit we are wrong, and ask Him to help and forgive us. But before we do anything at all we must be aware of what is right and what is wrong and whether we've been following the Torah's high standards. Before beginning to pray or at other moments during the day I try to take a few moments of quiet contemplation. I remind myself that only G–d is in control and that I can always turn to

Him for help and this helps me deal with my impulse to control others.

Reviewing my personal inventory gives me an awareness of every part of my life including my wrongdoings. The purpose of promptly admitting things we've done wrong is so that we can get beyond them. Wallowing in anger or guilt over deeds either done or not done helps no one. Even if I pray only once a day (my minimum obligation as a woman), this limits the duration of my guilt to twenty-four hours.

The Wisdom of Daily Prayers

The way the daily prayers are organized, we first praise G-d and recognize His greatness. First we acknowledge His control of the world so that we can relinquish our control and turn to Him for help. Since awareness of our shortcomings must come before we can ask for forgiveness, we ask G-d for wisdom, insight, and discernment.

"You graciously give man wisdom and teach insight to a frail mortal. Graciously give us wisdom, insight, and discernment. Blessed are You, G-d, gracious Giver of wisdom" (*Shemoneh Esrei* daily prayer).

Once G-d's power is acknowledged we then ask Him to bring us closer to Him and to the ways of Torah.

"Bring us back, our Father, to Your Torah, and bring us near, our King, to Your service, and influence us to return in perfect *teshuva* before You. Blessed are

You, G–d, Who desires *teshuva*" (*Shemoneh Esrei* daily prayer).

As we follow the prayer's organization we now ask for forgiveness for the things we have done both intentionally and unintentionally.

"Forgive us, our Father, for we have done wrong unintentionally. Pardon us, our King, for we have will-fully sinned. For You pardon and forgive. Blessed are You, G–d, the gracious One Who pardons abundant-ly" (*Shemoneh Esrei* daily prayer).

Daily prayer done with self–awareness provides an opportunity to ask for forgiveness each day with an awareness of what we have done wrong and a desire to improve our ways.

It is no wonder that the daily prayers end by hav-ing us express our gratitude and thanking G–d. What a gift we have been given in the opportunity to connect to G–d! I can leave my prayers knowing that I have considered my personal inventory of good qualities and bad ones and admitted my wrongdoings. I can unburden the weights of conflict and guilt. I can find the strength to right my wrongs and continue my life.

My tendency to get angry easily and cling to my anger was something I wanted to change. Deciding that I did not want to follow this pattern anymore only made me more aware of my anger. However, I still could not prevent this very powerful emotion from erupting. The attempt to change my tempera-ment was doomed because I was trying to control the outbursts but had *no* idea how to free myself of the anger within me.

Then I seized upon the idea of asking for G–d's help during prayer. I did this for about a year and gradually began to perceive a change in myself. It was not a matter of simply controlling my anger, but, indeed, I was not as easily angered as before. The little things in life were gradually losing their ability to make me as angry. Each situation was put back into perspective. When I do get angry, I pause before saying or doing anything. I think about why I am feeling angry. If, after I evaluate the reasons very carefully, I decide that I can calmly express the reasons for my anger, I do. But by walking away without a fight or argument, I protect and nurture my relationships. I can accept being wronged and deal with the conflict without being so angry and out of control as I had been in the past.

Taking stock of how I am as a person has become part of my daily routine. Becoming more aware of my shortcomings, I can now admit them more readily. In addition to forming a plan for overcoming them, I now ask G–d for help. I add these newly discovered shortcomings to my list of traits that I am trying to improve. At the same time, regardless of my actions, I have learned to accept and value myself. If I did not accept and value myself, taking an inventory would be too painful.

When we take a daily personal inventory, each

day becomes an opportunity to grow in both our awareness of ourselves and our awareness of the world around us. Each day is an opportunity to turn to G–d, as we admit our mistakes and ask for His help. Gradually, over time, we will be able to accept as G–d's will the things that we cannot change, and the ways of the Torah will become our way of life. When we make moral choices based on our knowledge of G–d and His ways in the world, we will be choosing to live according to G–d's will instead of our own.

Step Eleven

Sought through prayer and meditation to improve our conscious contact with G-d as we understood G-d, praying only for knowledge of G-d's will and the power to carry that out.

✦ ✦ ✦

Using Prayer
and Meditation

Since it's such a difficult process—and even though we are already on Step Eleven—we still continue to take personal inventory. Through serious introspection, we review our daily actions and try our best to avoid falling into old patterns. We have learned that prayer helps us connect with G–d. In Step Eleven, we continue to explore the impact of prayer and meditation in our search to improve our contact with G–d.

Step Eleven

Sought through prayer and meditation to improve our conscious contact with G-d as we understood G-d, praying only for knowledge of G-d's will and the power to carry that out.

We use prayer as a vehicle to reach G–d, we pray only to understand His will and carry it out.

In Psalms (3:4–5) there is a reference to this: "You,

G–d, are a shield about me…With my voice I called out to G–d and He answered me."

I had many questions when I began to take prayer seriously:

✦ What happens when I pray?

✦ Is prayer simply a shopping list of requested items?

✦ Will I get what I asked for?

✦ What if I don't get what I want?

✦ How do I meditate about something which I do not even have the mental capacity to know?

✦ Can I really have conscious contact with an infinite existence?

When we pray, we are speaking to the Creator and Master of the universe. We are making conscious contact with the one all–powerful Force in existence. Just the thought that we frail temporal beings could connect with the Infinite Power of the universe is astonishing.

Do we dare have the audacity to approach G–d and attempt to build a relationship with Him? In fact, the Torah tells us that we are obligated to do this, to study His words and pray to Him directly each day.

Moshe had the closest connection to G–d of any human being and even he felt a desire to know Him better. When Moshe was informed of the proximity of his death, he pleaded for his continued life. He not only wanted to be able to cross the Jordan into the Holy Land, but he also wanted more time and an opportunity to know G–d. "Oh my Lord, G–d! You have only begun to give your servant insight into Your greatness and Your mighty hand" (Deuteronomy 3:24).

Moshe was a great man, quite capable and accomplished, yet he managed to remain extraordinarily modest and devoted to G–d. Many of us believe that we can do everything by ourselves, either alone or with the help of other human beings. However, this point of view leaves no room for G–d. When we ask for G–d's help, this is an admission that we can't do it by ourselves, even with the help of others. We are deflating our egos. We are humbling ourselves and making space for G–d. Then we still do all that we can, while relying upon G–d as our partner.

Rambam notes that one ought to devote oneself to understanding science or other studies which will enrich one's knowledge of G–d (*Mishne Torah*, Sefer Hamadah, Hilchot Teshuva 10:6).

By daily study and observation, I try to sharpen and deepen my vision of what exists and what could be in both myself and the world. I study Torah and meditate on its concepts. I explore and learn about the natural world that G–d created. Interaction with teachers and trusted friends helps clarify my ideas. When I work the Steps with others, I share my ideas and am exposed to new insights. Ultimately, however, I must turn to G–d for guidance.

By daily prayer and meditation on what I have

learned, I am becoming more and more aware of a Power much greater than I. I am improving myself and my conscious contact with this Higher Power.

For me, meditation means taking time to think about some of the things that I have learned and contemplating my actions. It means taking time to sit quietly and focus on my inner thoughts and feelings, particularly before I begin to pray. I try to quiet all of my extraneous thoughts, so that I can become totally aware that I am about to stand before G–d and I think about the ideas that I want to express.

Personal prayer helps, even if I do not get the exact items on my shopping list. Prayer is a powerful tool of inner change and it connects me to the Source of everything that exists.

Sometimes an event or idea that helps to resolve a difficult situation occurs after I pray. I have asked G–d to help me know how to effectively communicate. After praying, I found the words that I needed. I have asked for help when I have felt overloaded and overwhelmed, not knowing what to do first. Praying helped me find the clarity and strength to continue.

Many times I did not get what I wanted. Did I ask for something that G–d knows would not be good for me? I wondered if I didn't yet know what to ask for?

I used to ask for many things in my personal prayers. Now I focus on asking for knowledge of G–d's will and the power to carry it out. I ask for G–d's help in coming to know Him and His will.

This is a big change. I had always believed that if you work hard, you get what you want, with or without prayer. Life's disappointments and tragedies have taught me otherwise.

As I mentioned previously, I was a teenager when my cousin Ezra suddenly became sick, blind, and brain damaged. My conclusion at that time was that if G–d existed—and I was not convinced that He did— then He wasn't a fair or kind G–d anyway. After all, Ezra was a good person who did not get what he wanted or deserved. The family prayed and prayed for his recovery, but he never recovered.

There were other disappointments in my life. I planned to be a super teacher, but could find no good jobs. I wanted to have a lot of children. I had only one child, but thank G–d, she is terrific. I was building a wonderful adult relationship with my mother, and then she died. I realize now that I do not have control over anything that happens, and just because I want something does not mean that I am going to get it. So, what kind of G–d is this, and what kind of system did He create for the world?

It has taken me many years to begin to understand. I cried and struggled. I studied and participated in lectures, meetings, and discussions. I prayed.

G–d is all powerful, all knowing, and all good. For every one of us He has created a purpose. However, the purpose is spiritual, *not* material. The real joy we get from life will be based on what we know and what we do with that knowledge, *not* on what we have. The ultimate reward is not even in this life, but in the next life. Although we may not always receive what we want, we will get what we need. Our relationship with G–d is based on being conscious of our actions, not habitually reacting out of instinct.

Formalized daily prayers have new meaning for me, because in them I am asking for what I need to know G–d better. Each day I pray for knowledge of G–d's will and the power to carry that out.

We differ from animals in many ways. An animal, for example, does not need to pray for knowledge of G–d's will. Its entire nature is created according to G–d's will, so that its actions are in line with G–d's plan for them.

Human beings have free will, because we were created by G–d with both an intellect and a physical body. We can choose to bend our wills to that of G–d's, or we can choose to run from G–d's will and pursue other desires.

In the book of Kings I, we are told that King Solomon asked G–d for wisdom. In addition to wisdom, G–d also gave him wealth and honor. Just like Solomon, I am not in this life alone. I also can ask for wisdom and for knowledge of G–d's will. I may not get wealth and honor, but with G–d's help, I will receive what I need in order to grow in my knowledge of G–d and of His world. As a bonus I have discovered more joy in my life since I have begun to live connected to the Source of all life.

By using prayer and meditation we can become different human beings. We can change our lives.

Step Twelve

Having had a spiritual awakening as the result of these Steps we try to carry the message to others and to practice these principles in all our affairs.

◆ ◆ ◆

Sharing Our Spiritual Insights

Now is a good time to review the first Eleven steps and examine the path to spiritual awakening.

+ I was powerless and out of control.
+ I found a greater Power to restore my sanity.
+ I turned my will and my life to G–d's care.
+ I took a hard look at my moral traits.
+ I confessed my shortcomings to G–d, myself, and others.
+ I prepared to permit G–d to cleanse me of my character defects.
+ I humbly asked G–d to remove my spiritual flaws.
+ I remembered all those I had harmed and pre-pared to make amends.
+ I apologized or otherwise compensated all those I offended.
+ I continued to take personal inventory and ac-knowledged new wrongs as soon as I became

aware of them.

✦ I prayed and meditated on a regular basis so that I could solidify my link to G–d, always trying to be closer to Him, to understand His will, and to carry it out.

In Step Twelve, we share all we have learned with others, applying the Twelve Step principles to our daily lives. For many people, it takes a long time before they can consciously do this step.

Step Twelve

Having had a spiritual awakening as the result of these steps, we try to carry this message to others, and to practice these principles in all our affairs.

Although we have reached the culmination of working the Steps, we have really just begun. Reading through the Steps once prepares one to return and go through the Steps one at a time, sincerely trying to accomplish the goals of each and every step. Each step helps to heal our lives. We may work for a longer time on one step or another, perhaps returning often to a particular step. Together the Twelve Steps will help one build a better life.

In Psalms there's a section very appropriate to this idea. We ask G–d to remove our wrongdoings and allow us to be teachers: "Hide Your face from my sins, and blot out all my wrongdoings. Create a pure heart for me. Renew within me a spirit of correctness. Do not cast me away from Your Presence, and do not take away Your Holy Spirit from me. Restore to me the joy of Your deliverance and with a generous spirit, support me. Then I will teach wrongdoers Your ways and sinners may return to You" (Psalms 51:11–15).

First we help ourselves. Only once we feel at peace, can we turn to helping others. As G–d supports us, we turn to support others. We receive kindness and generosity from G–d and we can act with kindness and generosity towards others. The process of *teshuva* or turning towards G–d is not complete until we can focus on both ourselves and others.

The message is built into the Steps: The only power is G–d. Any improvement happens with G–d's help. I pray to know G–d's will, to be able to carry it out and grow closer to Him. This means letting go of the reactive control, anger, and negativity. Then it is possible to act in a state of awareness with forgiveness, gratitude, acceptance, and a positive attitude.

I struggle to know G–d's ways so that I can practice them in my life and teach them to others. G–d's ways are filled with *chesed* or acts of kindness and generosity. This way can also be my way, if I perform acts of kindness and generosity as service to G–d and His creations. As a codependent, I tend to focus my attention and energy on controlling people and tending to their needs. I must make sure that my actions help others and serve G–d, instead of serving my need to be needed or in control. Then my actions can bring me closer to G–d.

Through all of the Steps, I have discovered a different kind of power, the power to be who G–d intended me to be: a person who strives for self improvement and strives to know G–d and do His will, thereby building a more satisfying life. I try to acknowledge my strengths and accept my weaknesses.

Instead of the illusions and fantasies that I see in society at large, the truths of the Torah and its way of life are beginning to guide my actions. I am becoming more complete. Now, what can be done with all this knowledge and power?

American society focuses attention on physical pleasures. Commercials, advertisements, movies, television, and books bombard us, shouting messages that we need more money, power, excitement, and beauty in our lives.

✦ Win the lottery! ✦ Buy new clothes! ✦ Have cosmetic surgery! ✦ Trade in your car! ✦ Trade in your house! ✦ Trade in your spouse! ✦ Color your hair! ✦ Lose weight fast!

Instead of buying into these empty promises, I have discovered another life—a spiritual life. The minute I walk away from my books, meetings, synagogue, or house, I re–enter the so–called "real world." This is not the world of the spirit, but the world of physical comfort and pleasure.

How will I survive as a spiritual human being? Do

I need to isolate myself and limit my encounters to only spiritual people? Is this desirable or even possible?

Each person must make this personal decision. The right choice will be different for each individual. For some people, living in a spiritual community and limiting encounters with the outside world is the right choice. Throwing away or limiting television, radio and newspapers protects a person from corrupting influences.

Although a more risky option, I choose to remain involved with the world. Jews are dispersed through-out the world and are obligated to serve as a light unto the nations. As the prophet Isaiah tells us, "I the Lord have called you in righteousness, and will hold your hand, and will keep you, and give you for a covenant of the people, for a light unto the nations" (Isaiah, 42:6). So, too, I believe I can try to serve as a light to all the people I meet. I do this not by lecturing or prose-lytizing but by acting with *chesed* (kindness and generosity) towards others, basing my behavior on Torah principles.

Choosing to be involved with the larger non-spiritual world has to be balanced with taking care of myself. I do not live in a religiously isolated community. Sometimes I need to remove myself from the materialistic American society. I need a break from mass media, and also necessary social/business engagements. Planning time for meetings with people who share my ideas and who support me gives me the understanding and strength that I need. These include formal Twelve Step meetings like Codependents Anonymous (listed in local papers or located by contacting the appropriate national group), study groups, lectures and informal gatherings with friends.

There are three connections that I have tried to form in my life: my connection to G–d, to myself, and to other people. Study, meditation, and prayer not only help me personally but strengthen my connection to G–d. I have made some decisions about who I need to be and have asked G–d for help. How I act with others, in fulfillment of Step Twelve, will be the true test of who I am.

As I practice the principles of the Twelve Steps within the Torah's framework I see the world as a place for me to learn and grow. I'm learning how to control my emotions and remain calm enough to handle difficult circumstances. I am trying to change into a person who thinks and then acts, and these actions are ones that serve G–d's will. I pray that these changes in me will have a positive effect on others. I know I still have a long way to go. Being kind to myself allows me to be kind to others.

My daughter and I were reading a story about a woman who gave so much to everyone around her that she never had any time for herself. I told my daughter that we would probably turn the page and find that she died at a young age. Sure enough, on the very next page, we were informed that she died very young. My daughter told me, "Mommy, she really should have taken care of herself first." A codependent compulsion to help others is not true *chesed.* You cannot serve G–d if you destroy yourself through your efforts to help.

I took care of myself by deciding to continue learning—by going out and studying Torah with others. Taking care of myself in this way was taking care of my daughter. My daughter learned that it is okay to take time for yourself. As I withdrew my constant "help," my daughter and husband proved to be capable of taking care of many things without me.

The Torah provides wonderful models. The *midot* of our ancestors, which we can emulate, continue to influence us today. They paved the spiritual paths and made it easier for us to travel these paths. We can help keep these paths clear and make it easier for others.

Our great rabbis and teachers taught through their actions. They were models of kindness and righteousness. Our rabbis tell us that if we want to learn Torah, we should listen to the words and observe the actions of our sages. When we have learned to follow their example, we also can be good role models.

The more we apply Torah principles to our lives and work the Steps into our daily affairs, the easier it will become to continue this practice. We can continue to change and move toward G–d and we can help others on their path. Together, humanity can embrace being truly human, basing our lives on knowledge and truth, deliberately choosing what we know is right and doing G–d's will.

It is possible to deliberately make good choices that clarify our knowledge of G–d's will, strengthen our connection to His wisdom, and increase our happiness. We can base our lives on knowledge of what is good, rather than be slaves to our physical desires for comfort, pleasure, wealth, and power. Through acts of kindness and generosity each individual can help to improve this world. G–d's gift to each of us is the ability to freely choose to follow His way to a happier life.

Step Twelve tells us that having had a spiritual awakening as the result of these steps, we try to carry this message to others, and to practice these principles in all our affairs. Step Twelve develops naturally from the other steps. How will you know if you've had a spiritual awakening? When you realize that the Steps have become so integrated into your life and your way of thinking that they have become your new habits.

Working all the Steps will change you just as following the ways of Torah changes and influences your thoughts, speech, and action. When these principles become a part of you and your life, you will carry this message to others and practice these principles in all your affairs. In the end, all your decisions will be based on your knowledge that only G–d is in control and He is there to help you. Gradually you will substitute His will for yours and be able to humbly ask for His help. Without pause you will also be able to look at yourself and rectify your wrongdoings. All of this will happen as you work the Steps. Even if you are unsure that you are ready to share what you have learned with others, your new way of living will automatically help those around you. In fact, the message of the Twelve Steps is carried best by someone who simply lives the Steps. A person who can integrate the ideas of the Steps along with the ideas of the Torah can be a powerful model and may be able to help others simply by the example of how they live.

The Twelve Steps are about change, about starting over as people who make deliberate moral choices based on knowledge of themselves, the world, and G-d, while coming to understand His will for them. As we make these changes in ourselves, we draw closer to G-d and become more satisfied with our lives. As we recover from bad habits and addictions, our healthier lifestyles will have an impact on those around us. We start with trying to improve ourselves. Who knows how far reaching the effect could be?

Prescription For Life

In the first chapter, I presented my prescription for life:

♦ Learn Torah ♦ Take Twelve Steps
♦ Call G–d in the Morning

This is not a glib formula, but an easy way to remember the key ingredients necessary to heal our souls and improve our lives. However, this is not a short-term prescription. We don't swallow it each day for a week and then resume our usual activities. Rather, this prescription must be internalized, made a part of us, day after day, month after month, year after year. We may have to take different dosages, as the circumstances of our lives change, but the basic prescription will remain unchanged.

The third phase of this formula, Call G–d in the Morning, referring to regular prayer, is one of the most crucial, as we find in Psalms 62:9:

"Trust in Him at all times, people. Pour out your

hearts before Him. G–d is a refuge for us."

Trusting G–d may be gradual and will grow as your relationship with Him grows. In his book, *The Art Of Jewish Prayer*, Rabbi Yitchok Kirzner compares trust in G–d to trust that develops between two people as follows:

"Trust between two people is built primarily in three ways: First, it is an outgrowth of the history of a relationship. If a wife has found her husband to be generally caring and loving over a variety of situations and over a long period of time, then she learns to trust him. Second, the more one does for the other, the more the recipient learns to trust the giver. Third, trust is furthered through communication. The more two people share their inner thoughts and feelings with each other, the more trust is fostered between them. Just as these three elements foster trust between people, they are factors in how we learn to trust G–d."

We can use this formula for building trust in our relationship with G–d. We can build a history with G–d, recognize that He is our giver, and communicate with Him by following His commandments, becoming more aware of His gifts to us, and by praying.

When I pray, I am serving G–d, but I am also benefiting myself. G–d does not need my prayers. I need to pray. Prayer serves many purposes. It reminds me that G–d is in charge, not me. It reminds me that I am not alone—I can always ask for help from the Source of everything that exists. It reminds me that I have a direct connection to G-d and helps me strengthen this connection. Through prayer, I contemplate different aspects of G-d's goodness and wisdom. I increase my knowledge of what is true and right and improve my character because the prayers tell me what is important and for what I should be asking. Prayer reminds me that my purpose in life is to gain that knowledge of what is true and right, so that I can come to know Him, thereby attaining the good life here and in the World to Come.

The good life is usually described as getting what your heart desires. The secular world may tell you that this means getting material goods and physical pleasures. In the *Mishne Torah* Rambam tells us that our hearts' desires should be coming closer to G-d. This closeness is what will ultimately give us happiness in this life and in the world to come. Prayer is our way to communicate with and draw closer to G-d.

The Torah relates G-d's request that we pray every day. In Rambam's *Sefer Ahava*, the Book of Adoration, we are told: "To pray daily is a positive commandment, as it is said, 'And you shall serve the Lord, your G-d' (Exodus 23:25). The service referred to, according to the teaching of tradition, is prayer, as it is said, 'And to serve Him with all your heart' (Deuteronomy 11:13). The sages commented on this, 'What may be described as service of the heart? Prayer'" (Hilchot Tefilla 1:1).

We are commanded to pray daily according to our

abilities. This includes all men and women, free or enslaved, rich or poor, educated or uneducated, those with great ability and those with less ability. We are to praise G–d, ask for what we need, and then thank Him.

Rambam explains that: "The obligation in this commandment is that every person should daily— according to their ability—offer up supplication and prayer, first speaking praises of G–d, then, with humble supplication and petition ask for all that they need, and finally offer praise and gratitude to the Eternal for the benefits already given in rich measure" (Hilchot Tefilla 1:2).

Males over the age of thirteen are obligated to pray three times a day, and according to the Magen Avrohom, women are obligated at least once a day. (Some opinions say twice a day, morning and afternoon.) This obligation gives one the opportunity to turn to G–d each day. Thus when we maintain this obligation we are keeping a regularly scheduled appointment with G–d. When we use the formalized prayers of the *Shemoneh Esrei*, we are praying for the very things that we need to improve ourselves. This is why it is helpful to follow the specific prayers of our traditional liturgy. In prayer we can also ask Him for knowledge of His will and the power to carry it out. We can call on G–d whenever we are in need.

I recently traveled to Israel on a late night flight. When you are traveling East, you lose time, and morning arrives very quickly. As the sun began to rise, so did the people. For the first time, I saw what Maimonides was talking about. There they were—the old and the young, men and women. Men with beards and clean shaven, black hats, kippahs and baseball hats. Women with wigs, hats, scarfs and all varieties of hair styles. The men gathered in various corners of the plane to form groups of ten, often with strangers. But they were not really strangers. They were one people, one family, who just did not happen to know each other. Most women stood by their seats. All of the people got up in their own time, washed, and prayed. As I stood by my own corner at the emergency exit, I realized that I, too, was a part of this family that just may not know each other. I am part of the group of young and old, men and women, who rise in the morning to connect with the Master of the universe.

If recited with concentration and intention, which is described in Hebrew as *kavana*, prayer can lead to an ongoing awareness of G-d, His will and our place in this world. The words of the formalized *Shemoneh Esrei* prayers have great meaning and purpose. *Kavana* is so important, that Rambam warns us that the words we say are not considered prayers without our concentration. Better to delay prayers than to say empty words.

Any prayer uttered without mental concentration, we are told by Rambam, is not prayer. If a service has been recited without such concentration, it must be repeated devoutly. If a person finds that his thoughts are confused and his mind is distracted he may not pray until he has recovered his mental composure. Therefore, on returning from a journey or if one is weary or distressed, one shouldn't pray until his mind is composed. The sages said that in this case one should wait three days until one is rested and one's mind is calm, and then one can recite the prayers.

"What is to be understood by concentration of the mind? The mind should be freed from all extraneous thoughts and the one who prays should realize that he or she is standing before the Divine Presence. Therefore, one should sit awhile before beginning to pray, to focus one's mind, and then pray gently, beseechingly, and not regard the service as a burden which he is carrying and which he will cast off and proceed on his way. One should also sit awhile, after concluding the prayers, and then leave. The ancient saints would pause and meditate one hour before the service, one hour after the service and take one hour in its recital" (Hilchot Tefilla 4:15–16).

Rambam describes an ideal state for prayer. I use it as an encouraging example. I know that prayer is good for me, even though I am not in such an exalted state of mind as Rambam describes. I try to concentrate with *kavana* according to my abilities at that moment. Sometimes I can concentrate without any problem and at other times it's more difficult.

Prayer has helped me get healthier in many ways. I noticed that when I say the formalized morning prayers, I feel calmer and more focused throughout the day. I recently lost both parents, and my grandmother came to live with us. There is a lot of extra work, including organizing and paper work, that now needs to be done. When I start to feel overwhelmed, I ask G-d for guidance. Just the asking gives me a feeling of relief. I remind myself that G-d's ways are always for the best and that he never gives anyone a burden that is too hard to handle. So, I try to be satisfied with all of my life, even the difficult parts, since it all comes from G-d.

Prayer can lead to personal change and to *teshuva*. When we pray, we are enlisting the help of the Eternal Source of all help. Daily prayer can lead us away from focusing on the physical, material world and help us focus on our spiritual lives and on the many gifts G-d gives to us.

Choose Life

You have just learned about what may seem to be an enormous task—trying to follow the ways of Torah and working the Twelve Steps of recovery. Perhaps you are wondering: Is it worth the effort? Is it really possible to freely choose to start over on a difficult path to what promises to be a healthier life? Do we have free will to do G–d's will?

Free will is one of Judaism's basic concepts. However, it is not as simple as it may seem.

In Psalms we find the following statement: "G–d, from heaven, looked down upon these sons of man, to see if there was any man of understanding searching for G–d" (Psalms 53:3).

This verse implies that searching is useless unless you know what you are searching for. To choose, you need to know that you have a choice.

I struggled with the idea of free will or free choice. Rambam writes in the *Mishne Torah* that everyone has free will. Oddly enough, my initial understanding of free will made me unsympathetic and judgmental towards others. I thought it meant that if someone did something right, it was to their credit. If someone did something wrong it was entirely their fault. After all, it was their choice.

My initial understanding of free will seemed unreasonable. It seemed cold and harsh. Either Rambam was wrong (unlikely) or my understanding of free will was wrong.

I found help from Rabbi Eliyahu Dessler in his book *Strive for Truth* (*Michtav Me-Eliyahu*). In his essay, "The Nature of Free Will," he talks about "the *bechira* point" (point of free choice). We all make free will choices, but at different levels depending on where we are. If we do something habitually and can't recall ever choosing to do it, it is not a conscious choice. We make a choice only when we struggle over our options.

Rabbi Dessler writes, "*bechira* comes into play only when one is tempted to go against the truth as one sees it, and the forces on either side are more or less equally balanced" (*Strive for Truth*, part II).

Rabbi Dessler cites the example of a thief. If the thief is caught, his free will choice for good may come when he chooses *not* to shoot his way out. For me, to rob and shoot someone is not my free will choice because I am already conditioned that this is a wrong act. It is at the thief's *bechira* point, not mine.

Sometimes I know that I am at a *bechira* point, a point where both possibilities seem equally strong, when I feel confused about what to do. There may be two options and they both seem to be the better option. I was attempting to sell a house by placing an advertisement in the local newspaper. I was so sure that it would sell quickly, I took out an advertisement for only four days. When it did not sell, I looked into the possibility of crediting those days towards a longer package. A supervisor at the newspaper said that I could only use a partial credit. When I called the next week, I told this to a salesperson who gave me a price based on a credit of the total amount. I froze. Should I correct her? Perhaps she misunderstood what I had said? Would she get into trouble for charging me too little? Perhaps she did understand but gave me the full credit for another reason. It's a large organization; what seems like a lot of money for me is really nothing for them. I did not respond at that time but I thought about what I should do. After I let the confusion clear, I knew that I had to offer to clarify which was the correct amount. I could not passively cheat the paper any more than I could take money from a store or an individual. I called back the next day and was pleased to find out that the salesperson had checked with her supervisor who had given her permission to give me the larger credit.

Everyone has their own points of free choice. It's impossible to judge anyone for making what I feel is a bad choice. The good choice might not even be a possibility for that person.

I can choose only for myself. I have chosen to work the Twelve Steps. I have chosen to follow the commandments of the Torah and its guidelines. For me, choosing Torah means choosing life. It means choosing a life based on knowledge of G–d and His ways in this world instead of merely being physically alive.

I am capable of understanding and searching for G–d. If I react to the world only unconsciously, solely through my instincts, following the demands of my physical body, then I am not choosing to live as G–d intended humans to live. G–d gave me a mind with the capacity to grasp ideas and a body to put those ideas into action. Animals serve their bodies. Human beings have the capacity to have their bodies serve their minds. It is G–d's will that I strive to know and try to act according to the knowledge of His will. I try to do G–d's will by learning, praying, and following His commandments, thereby living according to His law. The benefit of serving G–d is mine. I am trying to become a spiritual human being who chooses to follow His will. Striving to come to know Him will give me a life that is based on drawing closer to G–d in this temporary life, and to eternal life in the World to Come.

In the first Torah portion, Bereshit, we are told that we do not have to be slaves to our desires. We can rule over them. The Torah tells us about two brothers, Cain and Abel. They both brought offerings to G–d. Abel and his offering were acknowledged by G–d because he brought the best of his flocks. G–d gave no notice to Cain and his offering because Cain brought whatever was around. He was more interested in indulging himself physically and doing whatever was comfortable and easy. Cain did not make any deliberate choice but acted completely automatically with whatever was readily available. Cain was understandably angry and depressed. Perhaps he did not understand that G–d expects human beings to think and make the choice to serve Him. G–d tells him and us that it is possible to be in control of our physical desires, if one really strives for this.

G–d said to Cain, "Why are you angry? Why are you depressed. Is it not so that if you move towards the good there is forgiveness but if you do not move towards the good you take your wrongdoings to the entrance of your grave (to your death)? *Desire is upon you but you can rule over it*" (emphasis added) (Genesis 4:6–7).

The Cain and Abel story gives us an example of the difference between serving G–d's will and serving our physical bodies with all of their urges and desires. Abel chose to serve G–d and build his connection to Him. Cain really didn't make a choice. That's why he was so disappointed in G–d's reaction. He also ignores G–d's advice and continues to follow his physical and emotional desires. Then in anger, Cain ends up killing Abel.

Developing ourselves mentally so that we can serve G-d instead of our physical and emotional desires is not easy. It requires both choice and effort as well as making G-d our partner.

The Twelve Steps have supported my choice of serving G-d. They have helped me do *teshuva*, turn towards G-d and a good way of life. In the Twelve-Step system, this change is called recovery. In Torah it is called *teshuva*. Change is only possible if I truly want and plan to change, all the while acknowledging that I cannot do it alone. In the Twelve Steps, I turn to a higher Power. Torah tells me that this Power is G-d. Change is an ongoing process that requires periodic introspection and reliance on G-d through prayer. In both systems, as I develop into a healthier person who can truly live life, I have a responsibility to help others.

Let Us Review the Twelve Steps:

✦ 1. We admitted that we were powerless over our own urges, and that our lives had become unmanageable.

This emphasizes that G-d and only G-d has true power.

✦ 2. Came to believe that a power greater than ourselves could restore us to sanity.

From this Step we admit that G-d is our Sustainer and we can always turn to Him for help.

✦ 3. Made a decision to turn our will and our lives over to the care of G-d.

G–d knows what we need while we often confuse what we need with what we want.

✦ 4. Made a searching and fearless moral inventory of ourselves.

Teshuva *must begin with an undistorted picture of our behavior.*

✦ 5. Admitted to G–d, ourselves and to another human being the exact nature of our wrongs.

Once we have taken a good look at ourselves, teshuva *continues with sincere confession.*

✦ 6. Were entirely ready to have G–d remove all these defects of character.

Teshuva *is possible only when there is a desire for change.*

✦ 7. Humbly asked G–d to remove all our shortcomings.

Again, we turn to G–d for help. He is the Power. Without G–d's help we cannot change. The world is designed the way it is so that we will turn to Him for help.

✦ 8. Made a list of all persons we have harmed and became willing to make amends to them all.

We can become caring members of G–d's creations.

✦ 9. Made direct amends to people we have harmed wherever possible except when to do so would injure them or others.

It is not enough to think about our wrongdoings. We also must act. G–d forgives us only after we have forgiven those who have wronged us and made amends to those we have wronged.

✦ 10. Continued to take personal inventory and when we were wrong promptly admitted it.

We will know that real teshuva has occurred if we act differently when we are faced with similar circumstances.

✦ 11. Sought through prayer and meditation to improve our conscious contact with G–d as we understood G–d, praying for knowledge of G–d's will and the power to carry out His will.

Approaching G–d is an ongoing process that must continue throughout our lives. It involves thought (learning and meditation), speech (prayer and speaking in accordance with His will), and action (following His commandments and acting in accordance with His will).

✦ 12. Having had a spiritual awakening as the result of these steps, we try to carry this message to others and to practice these principles in all our affairs.

Through our speech and through our actions, we can strengthen ourselves and influence others by living a life based on Torah principles. Then we can find joy in living.

Do we need the Twelve Steps? Do we need spouses, family, friends, study partners, or even Torah?

Yes, since without them we are like people wandering in a forest trying to find our way out. Although theoretically everyone can find the right path, the person with the flashlight and map has a much better chance and an easier journey than the person who travels alone and unaided. The Torah is both our flashlight and our map. Our study partners have different map–reading skills and will sometimes see things that we missed. Our loved ones make the trip more pleasant and comfortable. Sometimes they give us a reason to continue when we grow tired or discouraged.

The forest is immense with all sorts of sections. Some of them are safe. Some are fraught with danger. Some are enlightening and some are difficult and discouraging. There are many forces in this forest trying to lead us in the wrong direction. Other people who have worked the Twelve Steps can be of enormous help. They have already ventured to many parts of the forest. They can help us find better and safer places. Then we can be at peace, secure in the knowledge that G-d will help us find our way to Him.

We must always turn to G-d for help. As we say in our prayers when we call Him in the morning (in the *Ahavah Rabbah* prayer preceding the morning *Shema*):

"With an abundant love have You loved us, G-d, our G-d. With exceedingly great pity have You pitied us. Our Father, our King, for the sake of our forefathers who trusted in You and to whom You taught the decrees of life, may You be equally gracious to us and teach us. Our Father, the merciful Father, Who acts mercifully, have mercy on us, instill in our hearts to understand and explain, to listen, learn, teach, safeguard, perform and fulfill all the words of Your Torah's teaching with love. Enlighten our eyes in Your Torah, attach our hearts to Your commandments, and unify our hearts to love and fear Your Name, and may we not feel inner shame for all eternity. Because we have trusted in Your great and awesome holy name, may we exult and rejoice in Your salvation."

We are alive as spiritual human beings when we use our bodies to serve our minds and when we strive for knowledge of G–d and His will for us.

The Torah is both a light and map to help us find the path to life. The Twelve Steps provide a system that helps us follow the directions. Prayer gives us the opportunity to contact the very Source of our existence and help.

G–d encourages us to make the right choice. As it says in the Torah:

"I have set life and death before you, blessing and curse. Choose life, so that you may live—you and your descendants—to love G–d, your G–d, to hearken to His voice and to cling firmly to Him. For that is your life and the length of your days" (Deuteronomy 30:19–20).

I needed to know that it was in my power to make a choice freely. I learned that everyone has *bechira* points, points of free will to make the right and healthy choice even when the options seem to be so equal. Do I choose what is physically easier and more comfortable or do I choose what I have learned is right? Do I continue to try to control my daughter in my habitual codependent way or do I give her some space to be and love her for who she is? Do I automatically react in anger or do I choose to be calm? Do I react with an undue sense of pride or do I remind myself to thank G–d instead since everything comes from Him.

I came to realize that I could continue to exist by reacting in a habitual way just like animals and be intellectually and spiritually dead, or I could begin to make deliberate choices about my actions and how I wanted to be and become spiritually alive. I chose life as a thinking person who tries to direct my life towards truth and knowledge of what is right based on Torah and G–d's will. You have the tools to make the right choices in your life. May you be inspired to do so!

A Personal Note

Make changes! Do Teshuva! Start Over! Why?
We have to be able to answer this question if we are
to take on such an enormous task. We need to always
be aware of the purpose and keep our goals in mind.

Many of us spend our lives focused on jobs, families, food, entertainment, and perhaps avoiding
unpleasant situations. Our lives seem to be in motion
with no real direction.

I recently spoke to a friend about a movie character who was amusing, but seemed to have no purpose
in life other than just existing with an occasional
heroic act. My friend replied, "Yes, I often feel like that
is my life."

When I first became a *shomeret* mitzvot—observant of the Torah's commandments—some of my
friends and family began to call me a fanatic. One person even told me that I should see a psychiatrist. I
asked him if he was happy in his life. He replied that

he was not. I told him that I was happy and that per–
haps he should see the psychiatrist. He told me that he
was already seeing one.

Existing for no purpose other than a family, job,
physical comforts, and avoidance of pain is not enough
for me to feel that I am fully living in a meaningful way
as G–d intended. Animals can be happy by fulfilling
their physical desires, because that is their purpose in
life. My primary focus is beyond daily survival—I try to
enrich my mind and soul through following G–d's will.
I need to use my G–d–given abilities to choose to serve
G–d and the mental/spiritual aspect of my nature.

Striving to know G–d by searching for knowledge
and doing His will has given me the good life, a life that
is based on trying to understand G–d and His will and
building a relationship with Him. Using my mind that
was given to me by G–d in pursuit of Him gives me
great pleasure that is qualitatively different from the
physical pleasures I get from activities such as eating
and exercise. Those physical activities are even more
enjoyable now that I understand the significance of
taking care of myself physically so that I can do *teshuva* and become closer to G–d. My life has healthy goals
and a positive focus. I am choosing to be a person who
attempts to improve as a human being in order to form
a connection to G–d and to serve Him properly.

In the first chapter of *The Path of the Just* (*Mesillat
Yesharim*), Rabbi Moshe Chaim Luzzato explains
"man's purpose in the world." He writes: "The Sages

of blessed memory have taught us that man was created for the sole purpose of rejoicing in G–d and deriving pleasure from the splendor of His Presence. For this is true joy and the greatest pleasure that can be found…When you look further into the matter, you will see that true perfection comes only in union with G–d…The essence of a person's existence in this world is only to uphold commandments, to serve G–d and to withstand trials, and the world's pleasures should serve only the purpose of aiding and assisting them, by providing the contentment and peace of mind in order to free the heart for this required service."

As I came to recognize G–d and the many benefits He has bestowed on me, I began to learn to love Him. The more I love G–d, the more I want to learn. The more I learn, the more I understand. The more I understand, the more I want to do. The more I do, the more I come to love G–d. In this way I connect my life to the Source of life. I choose the good life, where my heart's desire is to draw closer to G–d as I gain in knowledge of Him and His ways, and I connect myself to the Source of goodness. I am happier because I have connected myself to the Source of happiness. Serving G–d is my purpose. It is why I was created.

The Basic Prescription

Learn Torah. Try to learn as much Torah as possible. Knowledge of the Torah is knowledge of G–d since He is the Source of knowledge. He is knowledge itself.

Take Twelve Steps. Try to put the ideas and knowledge of Torah and the Twelve Steps into practice. Those ideas and the presence of G–d are recognizable in life and in the world. Think and make choices. Strive to love G–d with a desire to do His will.

Call G–d in the Morning. Pray. Cry out to G–d for help. He is the Source of life and everything that is needed in life. He is both the Creator and the Sustainer of life. Only G–d has the power to make you a thinking, choosing human being. Only G–d has the power to help you live instead of merely survive.

Rabbi Daniel Goldstein, of blessed memory, shared a well-known story with me. A man meets a young yeshiva student and says, "I'll give you a dime if you can show me where this G–d of yours is." The student quickly replies, "I'll give you a dime if you can show me a place where G–d does not exist."

Beginning

Where to begin? Many rabbis and teachers say that it's best to start with what you can do. Try not to do so much that you feel overwhelmed. As people who work the Twelve Steps say, "Start with tiny baby steps."

May we all have the wisdom to strive to know G–d.

May we all have the power to carry out G–d's will.

May we all have the ability to say, "I choose life."

Information Sources
Suggested Reading

Twelve Steps and Twelve Traditions. Alcoholics Anonymous World Services, Inc. Box 459, Grand Central Station New York, New York, 1952.

Ben Avraham, Rabbi Yona of Gerona. *The Gates of Repentance (Shaare Teshuva).* English translation by Shraga Silverstein. Jerusalem — New York: Feldheim Publishers, 1967.

Davis, Avrohom. *The Metsudah Tehillim.* Brooklyn, New York: Metsudah Publications and Simcha Graphic Associates, 1983.

Dessler, Rabbi Eliyahu E. *Strive for Truth (Michtav Me-Eliyahu).* English by Aryeh Carmell. Jerusalem–New York: Feldheim Publishers, 1983.

Beattie, Melody. *Codependent No More.* San Francisco, California: Hazeldon Foundation, Harper publication, 1987.

Hirsch, Samson Raphael. *Chapters of the Fathers (Pirke Avos).* Jerusalem–New York: Feldheim Publishers, 1967.

Hirsch, Samson Raphael. *The Pentateuch (Chami-shah Chumshay Torah)*. New York, New York: The Judaica Press, Inc., 1986.

Maimonides. *Mishne Torah The Book of Knowledge (Sefer Hamadah), The Book of Adoration (Sefer Ahava)*. Edited by Moses Hyamson. Jerusalem–New York: Feldheim Publishers, 1981.

Kirzner, Rabbi Yitzchok with Lisa Aiken, Ph.D. *The Art of Jewish Prayer*. Northvale, New Jersey: Jason Aronson Inc., 1991.

Luzzato, Rabbi Moshe Chaim. *The Path of the Just (Mesillat Yesharim)*. English translation by Shraga Silverstein. Jerusalem–New York: Feldheim Publishers, 1966.

Machzor for Rosh Hashanah and Yom Kippur. Translated by Rabbi Nosson Scherman, Co-edited by Rabbi Meir Zlotowitz. Brooklyn, New York: Artscroll Publications, 1985, 1986.

Malbim, Rabbi Meir Leibush. *Proverbs Malbim on Mishley*. Abridged and adapted in English by Rabbi Charles Wengrov, based on original draft by Avivah Gottlieb Zornberg. Jerusalem—New York: Feldheim Publishers, 1982.

Twerski, Abraham J. M.D. *Let Us Make Man*. New York: CIS Publishers, 1991.

Twerski, Abraham J. M.D. *Life's Too Short*. New York: St. Martin's Press, 1995.

Glossary of Terms and Ideas

Avodah zarah: Idol worship.

Baal, Baalat (baalei) teshuva: A Jew who turns towards G–d and repents for previous actions.

Bait Hamikdash: The Temple of Jerusalem. Literally, House of Sanctity.

Bechira: Free choice.

Chesed: Kindness, goodness or giving.

Chet: Often translated as sin. Literally, missing the mark.

Chovato b'olamo: Duty or purpose in the world.

Eretz Yisroel: Land of Israel.

Gam zu l'tova: This is also for the good.

Hadevakim, Mudbak: Sticking, gluing, attaching, cleaving, adhering, connecting.

Halacha, Halachic: Jewish law, pertaining to Jewish law.

Kavana: Concentration or focus. In connection with prayer it refers to praying with full attention to the prayer.

Kosher, Kashrut: In accordance with the Torah laws for food.

L'haamin: To have faith or trust, to believe.

L'yedah: To know or have knowledge of.

Machzor: Holiday prayer book.

Matzui rishon: The First Cause, the Creator.

Mezuzah, mezuzot: Parchment containing the Shema that is placed on the doorposts of the house.

Midot: Character traits.

Mikvah: Ritual bath.

Mitzvah, Mitzvot: Commandments of the Torah.

Mussar: Constructive criticism or reprimanding for the purpose of improving character.

Olam Habah: The World to Come.

Parsha, parshat: Torah portion.

Rabbeinu: Our Rabbi or teacher.

Rebono shel olam: The Master of the Universe.

Rishonim: Early commentators on the Torah.

Rosh Hashanah: Jewish New Year. Literally, the head of the year.

Shabbat: The seventh day of the week designated by the Torah as a day of rest, dedicated to the service of G–d.

Shabbaton: Shabbat retreat.

Shechina: G–d's presence.

Shemoneh Esrei: Daily set of prayers, originally consisting of eighteen blessings, now nineteen.

Shofar: Ram's horn.

Shomeret: One who guards or watches over.

Shul: Jewish house of worship, synagogue.

Teshuva: Often translated as repentance, it literally means a turning to or a returning. Used in reference to a return to G–d and His ways.

Tachanun: Literally means supplication. It is the name of the prayer following the Shemoneh Esrei in which there is a plea for G–d's compassion for forgiveness and acceptance of our prayers.

Tamim: Pure or whole.

Tashlich: Prayer service in which we beseech G–d to figuratively cast our sins into the water.

Tefilla: Prayer.

Tikun: Fixing, rectifying, mending or repairing as in *Tikun Olam*—repairing the world.

Torah: Originally referred to the Five Books of Moses or Chumash. Now a generic term for Jewish teachings and laws.

Tzaddik: Righteous person.

Tzedaka: Good deeds or charity.

Yeshiva: Jewish day school.

Yesod hayesodot: The foundation of foundations, the basis of life.

Yirat Hashem: Fear or awe of G–d.

Yom Kippur: Day of Atonement.

Zehirut: Character trait of caution or watchfulness.

Glossary of People

Dessler: Rabbi Eliyahu Dessler, (1891–1954), Rabbi, teacher and leader. He was a follower of the *Mussar* movement, founded by Rabbi Israel Salanter. Rabbi Dessler's teachings were a combination of *Mussar*, Jewish religious philosophy, Kabbalah and Hasidism. His ideas were published by his students from his manuscripts and their notes in the three volume *Michtav Me-Eliyahu* (*Strive for Truth*).

Hirsch: Rabbi Samson Raphael Hirsch, (1808–1888), Rabbi, scholar, writer, educator, leader and champion of Jewish civil and religious rights in Germany during the nineteenth century. He was the first among Orthodox rabbis to stress traditional Jewish learning and observance combined with an appreciation for the positive ideas of the secular world. His classic commentaries continue to influence the Jewish world today. His works include commentaries on the Pentateuch, the Psalms, *Pirke Avot* and the Daily Prayer Book.

Luzzato: (Ramchal), Rabbi Moshe Chaim Luzzato, (1707–1746), Italian Kabbalist, poet and writer. His poetry had great influence on the development of modern Hebrew poetry. He was revered by Eastern European Jewry for his ethical work of *Mesillat Yesharim* (*The Path of the Just*).

Maimonides: (Rambam), Rabbi Moshe ben Maimon, (1135–1204), Rabbi, physician, and philosopher. He is well known and respected as an expert on Jewish Law. His letters sustained the Jews during the difficult times in Spain and his work continued to influence Jewish people throughout the ages. Some of his books are *Sefer Ha–Mitzvot, Mishne Torah*, and the *Guide to the Perplexed*. His is often referred to as the second Moshe (Moses), second only to Moshe Rabbeinu.

Rabbeinu Yonah of Gerona: One of the Rishonim, who are considered to be both authorities and embodiments of the Torah. Also called Rabbeinu Yonah, the *Tzaddik* (Saint). His work *Shaare Teshuva* (*The Gates of Repentance*) was written to awaken the soul to the fear of Heaven.